Finding the
HEART *of* JESUS
in Sickness
and Infirmity

ABOUT THE AUTHOR

Ronald Leinen, MSC, in his own words ...

I am a priest-member of the Society of the Missionaries of the Sacred Heart, a Catholic religious congregation. I was born in 1927 and ordained in 1957. At present, I carry on ministry in the vicinity of Aurora, Illinois, west of Chicago.

My credentials for writing this book are both professional and personal. Professionally, I have given spiritual counsel to many people suffering from physical or mental disorders during my ministry as a priest. I hold three scientific degrees: a B.S. in Chemistry from Marquette University, Milwaukee, WI; a M.S. in Biological Science from De Paul University, Chicago, IL; and a Ph.D. from the University of Missouri, where my field was comparative physiology. From the beginning of my graduate studies, I had a special interest in the chemistry underlying mental disorders and emotional disturbances.

From 1975-79, I was staff chaplain at State mental hospitals in Rhode Island and Connecticut. From 1979-83, I was chaplain at general hospitals in Ohio. From 1983-91, I was a Certified Alcoholism Counselor in Ohio. My current ministry includes almost daily visits to the sick at a local hospital.

It is my experience that there is no power greater than the compassionate love of Jesus for the sick and suffering. Faith in him brings not only consolation, but fosters healing of mind and body.

Finding the
HEART *of* JESUS
in Sickness
and Infirmity

RONALD LEINEN, MSC

A Publication of Magnus Press

A Publication of Magnus Press
P.O. 2666
Carlsbad, CA 92018

Finding the Heart of Jesus in Sickness and Infirmity

First Edition, 2002

Printed in the United States of America

LCCN: 2001095739

ISBN: 0-9654806-9-0

Publisher's Cataloguing-in-Publication
(Provided by Quality Books, Inc.)

Leinen, Ronald.
    Finding the heart of Jesus in sickness and infirmity /
Ronald Leinen. -- 1st ed.
    p. cm.
    LCCN: 2001095739
    ISBN: 0-9654806-9-0
    1. Sick--Prayer-books and devotions--English.
2. Jesus Christ--Devotional literature. 3. Church work
with the sick. 4. Diseases--Religious aspects--
Christianity--Meditations.   I. Title

    BV270.L45 2002   242'.861
                        QBI01-701201

---

08 07 06 05 04 03 02   10 9 8 7 6 5 4 3 2 1

COMFORT

Psalm 23:1-4

The Lord is my shepherd, I shall not want.

He makes me lie down in green pastures;

he leads me beside still waters;

he restores my soul.

He leads me in right paths

for his name's sake.

Even though I walk through the

darkest valley,

I fear no evil;

for you are with me;

your rod and your staff—

they comfort me.

TABLE OF CONTENTS

Introduction

Dry Bones

Lying in a hospital bed or house-bound by infirmity, it is only natural to feel what the prophet Ezekiel felt when he spoke long ago to a captive people whose sufferings had made them spiritless:

> The hand of the Lord came upon me, and he brought me out by the spirit of the Lord and set me down in the middle of a valley; it was full of bones. He led me all around them; there were very many lying in the valley, and they were very dry. He said to me, "Mortal, can these bones live?" I answered, "O Lord God, you know."

You get the feeling from Ezekiel's answer that he didn't think so. After all, Ezekiel, too, was a captive in Babylon. Life may have seemed to him little more than a valley of dead, dry bones. But in the very moment of his hopeless response to God's question, the answer came from God himself to give Ezekiel encouragement and a promise of renewed life:

> Then he said to me, "Prophesy to these bones, and say to them: O dry bones, hear the word of the Lord. Thus says the Lord God to these bones: I will cause breath to enter you, and you shall live. I will lay sinews on you, and will cause flesh to come upon you, and cover you with skin, and put breath in

you, and you shall live; and you shall know that I am the Lord" (Ezek. 37:1-6).

Just as Ezekiel and his fellow Jews were captives in a foreign land, so we may feel captive because of some illness. Ezekiel offered his people hope. God had not abandoned them. We who believe in Jesus know that he has a human heart capable of feeling what we feel, and the power to raise us up. He inspires us even while we lie in a hospital bed or are house-bound by infirmity.

This spiritual truth is consoling to those who suffer and to those who keep watch with them. Nevertheless, it would not do to underestimate the suffering of the sick or infirm. I, for one, have never found a false cheerfulness or the offering of platitudes to be helpful to me when I was impaired in mind or body. On the other hand, I did need encouragement. The mere fact that someone would come to visit me was encouraging. If that person could help me to find spiritual meaning in my suffering, that was even better.

Sometimes the best spiritual support comes from others who are experiencing the same infirmity. Once, when I was confined to a mental hospital to receive treatment for an anxiety disorder, I lived with many other priests who were troubled by one or another emotional disorder. We were aware that outsiders often did not understand us. Since we took our meals in a common dining room which we shared with visitors, we decided to play a joke on them. One of us led an imaginary dog by an imaginary leash to a place near our table and petted it on the head while another priest fetched a saucer with food and set it down before the imaginary dog. More than forty years later, I can still remember the lift we received from the reaction of the visitors. By our joke, we exorcised the demon of self-pity and achieved a deeper bonding among ourselves.

This is a book of reflections from my years as chaplain and my own occasional experience of physical or emotional disability. When I ministered to people who were sick and infirm, I was aware that I was ministering to Jesus. It was he who was on the bed of pain or in the wheelchair or stooped over with age.

The stories and dialogue in this book will enable you, the reader, to identify with the persons I portray. They are not case histories of particular individuals. They arise from a global overview of my experience in two State mental hospitals and three general hospitals over the years as well as a lifetime of observations of people's concerns in the face of sickness and infirmity.

Every chaplain brings to his or her ministry a point of view. As a priest-member of a Catholic religious order, the Missionaries of the Sacred Heart, my point of view is the spirituality of the heart, centered on the heart of Jesus. He identifies with us, from his heart, when we are wounded with sickness or infirmity, and it is his heart which strengthens and encourages us.

In the State hospital setting, I learned how to minister to people of every belief and even without religious belief. Later, I carried over what I had learned into general hospital ministry. I have learned to respect the consciences of those who believe differently than I do. I have found that there is always common ground, either a shared belief in Christ, or in God, or at least in the dignity and worth that all of us have as human beings. Though I know how to minister to people who are not Christian, I have chosen to write this book from a Christian perspective. It is my hope that this book will be of service to sick or infirm persons who believe in Jesus' concern for them.

The book is small, because those who are suffering often have limited strength even for reading. I begin and close the book with prayers, and each story concludes with a prayer. The spirituality of the heart belongs to the heart, and the heart finds truth and strength in prayer. The prayers are mine, but you may find them to be a guide for offering your own appeal to the compassionate love of God in Christ Jesus.

Pray also for me, an old and somewhat infirm former chaplain.

⤳ PRAYER ⤶

Lord Jesus, I pray for those who believe that they have become only dry bones, asking themselves, "Can these bones live?" I pray that they may believe your response:

"Thus says the Lord God to these bones: I will cause breath to enter you, and you shall live. I will lay sinews on you, and will cause flesh to come upon you, and cover you with skin, and put breath in you, and you shall live; and you shall know that I am the Lord."

Inspire them with your love as they read and meditate upon these pages. May they come to appreciate your compassionate love for them.

As the Letter to the Hebrews says, you became like us and are able to sympathize with our weaknesses (Heb. 4:15). I believe that you love us even when our infirmities make it difficult for us feel anything but distress. I believe too that you would bring us to be joyful and thankful in the midst of our afflictions. The basis of Christian joy is hope. By your grace, Lord, we can hope for peace and happiness in place of the struggles of the present time. Our hope rests on our faith—our belief that you are indeed loving and want to bring us to our destination, which is everlasting happiness with you.

I believe that you are powerful and can lead us to a more perfect union with yourself, if we are willing. Thank you for your past favors and your promise for the future. You have brought me and my suffering brothers and sisters through many difficulties, Lord Jesus. I believe you will complete the work you have begun. Thank you for your faithful love and care of all of us. Amen.

Chapter 1: Why Me, Lord?

We can go through life hearing about the catastrophes that happen to other people and be little affected personally. It may not occur to us that the same catastrophes can happen to us. When they do happen, an early reaction may well be, "Why me, Lord?" Of course, we are not being singled out. Sickness and infirmity are the common lot of humankind, together with their opposites: health and vigor. The condition of a particular person on a particular day may be one or the other.

God calls each of us to begin each day with abandonment to the divine will. If we trust in God, we are not alone. Curiously, sickness can be more conducive than health to our being able to begin the day with a prayer of trust. Whether we are sick or healthy, we gain most by seeing everything in our lives from a spiritual perspective. In sickness, we can gain a deeper faith; in health, we can gain a deeper spirit of thanksgiving. That does not mean that we cannot thank God for his gifts when we are sick. In that circumstance, however, thanksgiving rests entirely on our faith.

The goodness of God does not come and go with our physical or mental condition. It does not come and go with our earthly gains and losses. We can even have peace in the midst of difficulties if we have faith and humility. Humility is important because it enables us to see that our lives are entirely in the providential care of God and that we are all peers in the human condition. "Why me, Lord?"

comes from a temporary forgetting that we are all equally in need of divine help to reach our ultimate goal, which is beyond all earthly suffering. Along the way, we may be sick or infirm. Our worth depends not upon our being healthy but from the fact that we are all children of God destined for union with God in Jesus.

The heart of Jesus understands the pain of those who call out in their distress. He identifies with each and every one of us. He himself experienced the pain of the human condition. Jesus is most near when we call out, "Why me, Lord?" He then invites us to abandon ourselves into his care, to receive the peace that only he can bestow.

A MIDDLE-AGED MAN WITH INCURABLE CANCER

When George returned from his doctor's office, he was deeply depressed. Test results showed that he had cancer of the liver. A week later, exploratory surgery revealed that the cancer had spread to other abdominal organs as well. At the advanced stage of the cancer, surgical removal, radiation or chemotherapy were unlikely to help. George opted not to undergo the rigors of any treatment. He would simply live out his remaining months as best he could. The doctor had told him that soon he would need to be placed in an institution where he could receive a regular regimen of pain-killing drugs.

For many years George had not been particularly religious. In spite of having been raised in a devout Lutheran household, he practiced his faith in a hit or miss manner, attending church only several times a year. Even then he went solely to keep up appearances among his neighbors. One reason for his poor attendance was the fact that he was running a company which was just beginning to show a profit. That required ten-hour days at least six days a week, and often on Sunday.

His wife Sylvia had long been a kind of "widow." She received little more attention than George's religious practice. They had no children. There would be no heir to the business, and Sylvia would have to sell it if she could find a buyer. She found solace in her faith in Jesus. And she had remained a faithful churchgoer in spite of George's neglect of his religion. Sylvia took her marriage vows seriously and accepted the fact that she had a husband who neglected her. That was her cross. At least George had always been faithful to her. She had lived in hope that at some future date, when the business was better established, she and George would have more time to spend together. But it was not to be in the way that she had imagined. In the meantime, she entrusted herself and her marriage to the Lord.

As he sat in a recliner in his living room, George looked at a picture of Jesus which Sylvia had hung on the wall. The picture portrayed Jesus as the Good Shepherd. George began a conversation with the picture: "I feel like a hypocrite praying to you now, but I don't know what to do. I'll lose my company that I have worked so hard to build up. Sylvia will be a young widow. Both of us are in our forties. She'll probably marry again. I'll be buried, and maybe forgotten. There are no children to remember me. What am

I to do? Why are you letting this happen to me?"

A feeling of self-pity swept over George, and he despised himself for it. He had always been strong and in control of his life. His helplessness was so thoroughly unfamiliar that he turned again to the picture. "When I was a kid, my parents told me you were always loving. It is hard for me to believe that now."

As George brooded, something moved him to reach for the family Bible which Sylvia kept on a table near the recliner. He opened it at the 23rd Psalm:

> The Lord is my shepherd,
>> I shall not want.
> He makes me lie down in green pastures;
>> he leads me beside still waters;
>>> he restores my soul.
> He leads me in right paths
>> for his name's sake.
> Even though I walk through the
>> darkest valley,
> I fear no evil;
>> for you are with me;
>>> your rod and your staff—
>>>> they comfort me.
> You prepare a table before me
>> in the presence of my enemies;
>>> you anoint my head with oil;
>>>> my cup overflows.

Surely goodness and mercy
> shall follow me
> > all the days of my life,
> and I shall dwell in the house of the Lord
> > my whole life long.

When George looked up again at the picture, it seemed as though Jesus' penetrating gaze was a compassionate concern for him. It was not a look of pity, but rather a kind of loving demand that George take both Jesus and his faith more seriously for his own sake. In a way that George could not possibly explain even to himself, there came over him a feeling of peace and even a measure of acceptance of the trial of his illness. As he contemplated the tender love of Jesus, George realized that for the first time in his life he was going to have to learn to be a sheep. By the grace of God, he began to put his life into the hands of Jesus.

At first, George was astonished that he could feel so much peace even though he was dying of cancer. Then he understood that there was something far greater than his earthly ambitions at work in his life. He understood that a God to whom he had given only occasional fragments of his time and energy was truly concerned about him, that God had a heart. He saw that Jesus, indeed, is always concerned about those who wander, and is always ready to forgive. At that moment, George was able to let go of his anxiety and simply allow himself to enjoy the gift of peace.

⤚ PRAYER ⤙

Jesus foresaw that his apostles would have deep feelings of insecurity because of his passion and death. In the present day, when someone is sick and suffering, a question may arise in the sufferer's mind and heart, "If you love me as much as you said you do, Lord, how can this be happening to me?" Then he or she may remember that all whom Jesus loves have suffered, no one more than his own mother. Who then are any of us to complain? Yet we may still feel driven to complain, for none of us is as holy as Jesus' mother.

How hard it is to trust you, Lord! You yourself needed to trust your Father during your passion. Those who are desolate may find relief by thinking about your desolation on the cross. You were certainly a beloved Son. Yet you were allowed to suffer greatly and to be deprived of almost all human consolation. Only your mother and a few other disciples stood at the foot of your cross. You did not come down from the cross or ask your Father to take you down. You trusted in your Father's loving will for you and for us.

In our own trials, we may begin to think that you do not hear us in our need. We may ask, "Where is Jesus?" You are not surprised. You are patient with us as we struggle to understand and regain our confidence in your love for us. Isaiah said of you:

> *A bruised reed he will not break,*
> *and a dimly burning wick he will not quench (Is 42:3a).*

By your grace, we begin to see that you consider our learning to trust you more important than the passing suffering in our lives. How else could we learn to trust you except by enduring with faith during our present difficulties and all the others which may occur?

You are not indifferent to our suffering. You unite it with your own and make it holy. Then we can humbly ask you to support us during our trials. Speaking in your name, Isaiah said:

I hid my face from you
> *but with everlasting love*
I will have compassion on you,
> *says the Lord, your Redeemer (Is 54:8).*

For my part and on behalf of those to whom I minister, I believe your word, Lord Jesus. I abandon myself entirely into your loving care. May your mother who endured so much and yet never lost faith in you have compassion on us. Though she is now at your side in paradise, may she also abide with us and assist us with her presence and her prayers. Amen.

A MIDDLE-AGED WOMAN AWAITS MASTECTOMY

Helen pressed a button to raise the head of her hospital bed. She swung the tray table over her lap, reached into a drawer and pulled out a small mirror. Holding it before her face, she mentally asked herself, "What am I?"

The results of her tests had come back last month. Her doctor had said that her only hope for becoming free of cancer was a mastectomy. Helen was terrified of cancer. However, the doctor's words planted another feeling in her heart. If she went through with the operation, could she ever again be a whole woman? She visited another doctor to get a second opinion, and he confirmed what the first one had told her. Last night, she had checked in at the hospital for early morning surgery.

In the first moments after the second doctor had confirmed her worst fears, Helen was not thinking about God. Her concerns were for her husband, Charles, and their children. Helen was only 35 years old, happily married for fifteen of them. She and Charles had two teen-aged sons and an eight-year-old daughter. She loved being a wife and mother. She did not want to die so young and leave them abandoned.

Only later did she begin to think about God. She had been a good practicing Catholic all her life. She and Charles were raising their children in the faith and teaching them how to live as good Catholics. When she looked back at her teens, she was able to find moral lapses which she had long since repented and confessed, as a good Catholic is supposed to do. The priests had told her several times that when God forgives he is serious about it. The sins are gone. Why then this cancer and the wounding of her womanhood?

Now, lying in her hospital bed, she set down the mirror and picked up a Bible she had brought with her. The Bible had always been a powerful help for her when she was in distress. She found these verses:

> If I go forward, he is not there;
>
> or backward, I cannot perceive him;

on the left he hides, and I cannot behold him;

> I turn to the right but I cannot see him.

But he knows the way that I take;

> when he has tested me, I shall come out like gold.

My foot has held fast to his steps;

> I have kept his way and have not turned aside.

I have not departed from the commandment of his lips;

> I have treasured in my bosom the words of his mouth.

But he stands alone and who can dissuade him?

> What he desires, that he does.

For he will complete what he appoints for me;

> and many such things are in his mind.

Therefore I am terrified at his presence;

> when I consider I am in dread of him.

God has made my heart faint;

> the Almighty has terrified me;

If only I could vanish in darkness,

> and thick darkness would cover my face! (Job 23:8-17).

How easy it was to identify with Job in his sufferings, Helen thought. Like Job, she was not conscious of any current sins which could explain her illness and suffering. She had sinned, but that was history, and her sins had been forgiven. The one difference was that the testing of Job occurred at the hands of Satan. She saw no reason to apply that literally to herself. Life itself tests all of us. When the Father sent Jesus to restore what sin had lost, he sent him to save and heal, not to make people sick by putting them into the hands of Satan.

During her reflection, Helen wondered, "Why am I sick in the first place? Couldn't Jesus have prevented my getting cancer?" She knew from her life experience that good people often get sick, while people who are not good may enjoy excellent health. For example, her brother-in-law who was an absolutely impossible person—thoroughly selfish and rude—boasted that he hadn't had a sick day in his life. Yet one of her aunts, who was a paragon of virtue, had been sickly from her childhood. Knowing this truth in her mind, however, was not enough to satisfy her.

It was only later, when the hospital chaplain anointed her with the oil of the sick that she received the grace to accept the fact that Jesus does not usually stop us from getting sick, but rather strengthens us by the power of the Spirit. That power may indeed have a healing effect in our minds and bodies, and sometimes the Lord does work a miracle. Jesus will always heal our souls if we are open to his healing.

After the anointing, Helen began to experience the closeness of God's presence. She didn't understand the reasons for what was happening to her, but her faith in Jesus' love for her was strengthened. After the chaplain left, she looked at a little picture of the Sacred Heart which she used as a bookmark in her Bible, and she abandoned herself to Jesus. He would give her a wholeness as a person and as a woman far greater than any disfigurement from the surgery. Had he not already given her a husband and children who had promised to support her with their love, as a sign of his own?

Worry and fear began to ebb slowly away. In their place came a beautiful sense of peace, for she knew beyond a doubt that Jesus and her family would be faithful to her in the days, weeks and years to come.

⤙ PRAYER ⤚

Jesus went before us in bearing the disfigurements which life inflicts on us, and the contempt which we may fear will be the result. Isaiah prophesied concerning him:

> *...he had no form or majesty that we should look at him,*
> *nothing in his appearance that we should desire him.*
> *He was despised and rejected by others;*
> *a man of suffering and acquainted with infirmity;*
> *and as one from whom others hide their faces*
> *he was despised and we held him of no account (Is. 53:2b-3).*

Yet Isaiah introduces his description of Jesus' passion by proclaiming the glory and fulfillment concealed in it:

> *See, my servant shall prosper;*
> *he shall be exalted and lifted up,*
> *and shall be very high (Is. 52:13).*

When our bodies are violated, even by a necessary hurt to our whole-ness, we can feel only loss until Jesus gives us hope that he will make us whole again. He never promised to heal every bodily wound, but he did promise to raise us up in spirit even now, if we trust in him. He promised too that, some day, he will make us whole again in body as well as in spirit.

Therefore, Lord Jesus, I pray for all of your children who grieve over the bodily injuries which they must endure in this world. You understand their distress, not only because you are God but also because your own body was bruised and broken. When you anticipated your sufferings while at prayer in the Garden of Olives, your Father sent an angel to console you. Now, you send your angel to console those who trust in you.

Thank you for loving us so much that you not only laid down your life for us but continue through the ages to care for us tenderly. Inspire us with a deeper faith and hope. May our belief in your love for us and our love for you be our strength this day and every day of our lives. Amen.

A MOTHER GIVES BIRTH TO A BABY WITH DOWNS SYNDROME

It was early evening and the curtains were closed in the hospital room to which Joan had been taken from the obstetrical suite. From a nearby room, she could faintly hear the crying of a baby, a sound that should have brought joy because of its promise of new life which could be lived to the full. However, that morning Joan had given birth to a baby with Downs Syndrome. The doctor had diagnosed the defect during an examination in the sixteenth week of pregnancy. Because Joan and her husband Fred were devout Baptists, they never considered an abortion. A later examination indicated that the fetus was a girl. Joan now had a little girl who would never be normal and who would require constant care for many years to come. As she lay alone in her room, the crying of another woman's baby brought dread, not joy.

When Joan's obstetrician walked into the room, she prepared herself for the worst. For a silent moment, the doctor was visibly uneasy. Although she often had to bring bad news to the mothers of newborn babies, the doctor was always deeply moved when she fulfilled her professional task. All she could do was offer her one woman's compassion for another woman's plight. Feeling a great emptiness inside, Joan began to weep. She turned her face into the pillow. At that moment, she wanted to be alone. She had already named her little girl Jennifer. At the beginning of her pregnancy, Joan had entertained fantasies about playing with her daughter as she grew up. Now the games would always be a reminder of her daughter's disability. After a short while she turned again to face the doctor, thanking her for all that she and the other medical staff had done for her and the baby.

Fred waited outside the door until the doctor had completed her difficult duty. The doctor left the room, and Fred silently entered. Both Joan and Fred began to wonder, "Why us, Lord?" They had gone out of their way to avoid anything which could adversely affect the development of the baby she was carrying. They neither smoked nor drank nor used any other drugs. In every way, they had been careful to live healthy lives, in part because of their concern for the children they would bring into the world. They both wondered, "When we have done everything right, what more can we do?" It didn't seem fair that they, of all people, should have a child afflicted from birth. "Why is this happening to us?"

The pain and perplexity of Joan and Fred arose from their concern for Jennifer as well as for themselves. Jennifer would never be able to enjoy the gift of a normal life, and they would never be able to enjoy the growing up of a normal little girl. After the two of them had comforted one another and Fred had gone home for a short while, Joan remembered the Gospel story about Jesus blessing the children. She opened her bedside Bible to refresh her memory:

> Then little children were being brought to him in order that he might lay his hands on them and pray. The disciples spoke sternly to those who brought them; but Jesus said, "Let the little children come to me, and do not stop them; for it is to such as these that the kingdom of heaven belongs." Then he laid his hands on them and went on his way (Mt. 19:13-15).

Jesus was praising the children's simple trust in their parents' good will toward them, and their trust in him when their parents led them to him. Joan had a feeling that Jesus was reminding her of her own need for trust. Jesus had clearly shown that he loved little children. They were open to his love and guidance to a degree which he often did not find in their elders. They were ready to receive his blessing in this world and the next. As Joan thought about that encounter between Jesus and the children, she firmly believed that Jennifer was in his loving care and would be in his care during the years to come.

Through the peace which she was beginning to feel, Joan realized that Jesus was concerned about her also. He understood her grief, as he had once understood the grief of Jairus, a leader of the synagogue, whose only daughter lay dying (see Luke 8:41-42 and 49-56). When he entered our human world, he assumed all of its joys and sorrows. Jesus would be her spiritual support in her sorrow.

At the moment, Joan's world was indeed a place of tears. Yet, she was able to foresee that her love for Jennifer and her daughter's love for her could bring joy to both. Thus, Joan became willing to abandon herself and Jennifer to Jesus' care, and, with her encouragement, Fred too put himself and his family in the hands of the Lord. He and Joan needed to stop thinking about what they did or didn't do, and simply trust in the loving kindness of Jesus. For in Jesus both they and their daughter would find peace and joy.

⤚ PRAYER ⤙

When parents who really want their newborn baby are about to have a child who is severely impaired, they are confronted with a painful choice. While others follow the way of death, choosing abortion, Christians who faithfully follow Jesus' way of life need the strength their faith can give them to choose life for their child. It is natural for them to wonder how the Lord could let this happen to them.

For the worldly, sickness and infirmity are merely a bitter fate. For those who believe, they are a mystery hidden in God's love for his children. In his own afflictions, the psalmist prayed:

Why are you cast down, O my soul,
    and why are you disquieted within me?
Hope in God; for I shall again praise him,
    my help and my God (Ps. 42:11).

Lord Jesus, it would be unkind to tell parents like Fred and Joan, while they still keenly feel the pain of disappointment, that their child's disability is actually an opportunity. Nevertheless, that is what Jennifer's special needs can be for her parents. In ministering to their daughter, they will be ministering to you. You came into the world a healthy child, but you were still helpless. You needed the loving care of Mary and Joseph. Jennifer will need such attention during her entire life.

I pray that you may give to the parents of children who are impaired the wisdom to see you in their children. I pray that you may give them hearts that are moved by compassion to bring their children peace and joy. Reveal yourself to the little ones in the care of parents filled with your spirit, and bring them all closer to the everlasting union with you for which you have created us. Amen.

CHAPTER 2: I'M TOO YOUNG TO HAVE THIS ILLNESS

The shock of discovering that we have a serious illness which usually attacks people much older than ourselves is likely to throw our lives way out of balance. If the illness is life threatening, fear may pervade every conscious thought. We may even wonder if what is happening to us is a punishment from God. At such times we need to remember that people whose lives are not virtuous sometimes enjoy good health, while others who are innocent may suffer many illnesses. *Continued good health is not a measure of virtue.*

The stories below describe different kind of problems among people who believe they are too young to have a particular illness or infirmity. The young father who is awaiting open-heart surgery is amazed that he has heart disease at an early age. He is also worried about his family if he does not survive. Still, it is likely that he will live and have a relatively normal life after the operation. In contrast, the victim of MS and the young woman having a hysterectomy are not only surprised to learn of their conditions, but know they must rearrange their lives in depth.

Their consolation and their help is knowing that Jesus easily relates their suffering and their patience to his own experiences in his passion. He was stripped of his dignity and his life. He died in apparent failure. Yet he accomplished more for the world than anyone else who has ever lived. They will be close to his heart as they come to acceptance of their future and join their sacrifice to his. Then they will be able to pray with the Psalmist:

> As for me, I said in my prosperity,
>> "I shall never be moved."
> By your favor, O Lord,
>> you had established me as a strong mountain;
> you hid your face;
>> I was dismayed.
> To you, O Lord, I cried,
>> and to the Lord I made supplication:
> "What profit is there in my death,
>> if I go down to the Pit?
> Will the dust praise you?
>> Will it tell of your faithfulness?
> Hear, O Lord, and be gracious to me!
>> O Lord, be my helper!"
> You have turned my mourning into dancing;
>> you have taken off my sackcloth
>> and clothed me with joy;
>> so that my soul may praise you and not be silent.
> O Lord my God, I will give thanks to you forever
> (Ps. 30:6-13).

A YOUNG ACCIDENT VICTIM LEARNS THAT HE HAS MS

Ralph did not see the car backing out of a driveway until the last moment. A parked car next to the driveway blocked his view. When he caught his first glimpse, he instinctively moved his foot to the brake pedal. Physiologically speaking, his brain told his foot to step on the brake pedal. But his foot would not obey the command, and Ralph's car caromed off the back of the other vehicle, leaving a sizable dent in his right fender. At this point, his foot did find the brake pedal and he was able to stop. Both drivers got out and surveyed the damage. After exchanging insurance information, each went on his way.

Ralph was perplexed by his inability to stop more quickly. Why had his foot been so sluggish in responding? He decided to visit his doctor and have his right leg checked. His family doctor did not feel competent to diagnose him and sent Ralph to a neurologist, who did extensive tests at a local hospital. When the results came back, Ralph's own doctor called him with the startling diagnosis: early multiple sclerosis.

Ralph did not believe the doctor. The neurologist must have made a mistake. He decided to go to another specialist for a second opinion. Ralph was devastated when the second neurologist confirmed the diagnosis. He had nowhere to turn; he would have to face the truth.

Ralph had always considered himself a healthy young man. He was still only thirty years old and quite athletic, engaging in handball with friends at a local gymnasium. But now he was facing the progressive loss of the ability to control his body. Sooner or later, there would be no more handball with his friends; there might be no walking. Ralph knew that MS could strike the young, but how could it be him? He had a life to live. Now that life would slowly vanish like an elusive dream.

Perhaps he had waited too long to get married, but he had long intended to do so and have a family after he firmly established the small auto body repair shop which he had started. Now there would be no marriage in his future. He couldn't expect a woman to marry a man who might soon be greatly incapacitated. There would be no special lady whom he could cherish and who would cherish him. Nor would he be able to romp with the children who would never be. Others would have to do for him what any ordinary man does for himself, from bathing to feeding himself.

He had seen others with this disease and had a clear idea of what was in store for him unless a miracle happened. He didn't care whether the miracle was a medical breakthrough or a special act of God. He did not want MS to rob him of an active life. He was much too young for such a fate.

During the first couple of years after the discovery that he had an irreversible and crippling illness, as his condition deteriorated, Ralph began to grieve over the loss of control over his body. He moved back and forth between feelings of anger, unrealistic hopes and depression. As the years passed, his depression deepened as he progressed from needing a walker to needing a wheelchair. Eventually, he could not even move himself in the wheelchair.

He tried unconventional remedies ranging from acupuncture

to special diets. He frequented prayer meetings led by faith healers. When nothing positive happened, he simply brooded. Disappointment that God was not healing him alternated with intense prayer for a miracle. As the years passed, he gradually gave up his youthful hope for deliverance. He had not come to spiritual acceptance, but only to vegetative apathy.

But one day God began to get his attention as he listened to a cassette recording of the Bible and heard the passage where St. Paul talked about his own afflictions and hardships:

> We are afflicted in every way, but not crushed; perplexed, but not driven to despair; persecuted, but not forgotten; struck down, but not destroyed; always carrying in the body the death of Jesus, so that the life of Jesus may also be made visible in our bodies. For while we live, we are always being given up to death for Jesus' sake, so that the life of Jesus may be made visible in our mortal flesh (2 Cor. 4:8-11).

Ralph's thoughts turned to Jesus' crucifixion, for he had been nailed to a cross, where he was quite helpless. Like Ralph, he could move neither hand nor foot. Yet at the end, Jesus was able to say, "Father, into your hands I commend my spirit" (Lk. 23:46).

After Jesus died, his heart was pierced with a lance, opening it to all the world. What mattered most for Ralph was that Jesus' heart was open to him. He believed that Jesus understood what had happened to him, because Jesus had shared his predicament. He believed that Jesus loved him as he was.

Ralph prayed, "Lord Jesus, into your hands I commend by body, my spirit and my future." When he had offered this prayer, God's peace began to sweep over him. Ralph expected the feeling to be only temporary, but he was grateful nonetheless. In fact, that was the moment when he came to spiritual acceptance. From that time forward, he was only rarely tempted to thoughts of disappointment with the Lord or a sullen apathy over the debilitating physical condition life had dealt him.

When he was eventually admitted to a nursing home, he was no longer young. It was there that he discovered his gift for helping other residents and visitors to come to a deeper appreciation of the love of Jesus for them, whatever their circumstances might be. He found his own fulfillment, as Jesus had, fixed hand and foot to his own "cross," a wheelchair from which there was no escape.

But love is not bound by material objects. And the love of Jesus radiated from Ralph's presence whenever he shared his life with another person in need.

⊰ PRAYER ⊱

Lord Jesus, you have given us the ability to make plans for our future. These plans give us hope and pleasure. You have also given us a mortal nature which is subject to sickness and infirmity. When you allow these afflictions. I believe that what you want from us is abandonment to your will in every circumstance of life and at every age.

Living a virtuous life does not mean that we will not have problems. Both saints and sinners have problems. An ancient writer whose people had been conquered by a ruthless enemy wrote:

> All this has come upon us, yet we have not forgotten you, or been false
> to your covenant (Ps 44:17).

He then calls out:

> Rise up, come to our help. Redeem us for the sake of your steadfast
> love (Ps. 44:26).

It is not our fantasies but rather your loving plan for us which will
lead us to our fulfillment. When we are frustrated by ill health or other
obstacles which we cannot overcome, I believe that what seems impossible to us is not impossible for you. I believe too that you will do this in your
way, not ours, and that you will do it in your time. You awaken those who
are spiritually asleep. Then you call them to share in your ministry of
compassion as best they can. Thus, you gave Ralph an apostolate in spite
of his paralysis.

I believe that what you look for during our times of trouble is faith
that you will provide whatever is necessary. You also look for patience, for
we surely cannot have patience without faith. During our troubles, we
may ask, "Where is Jesus?" We may think that we know what your response
ought to be. However, you oversee this world and our lives in it with a creative and uplifting power based on a long view of what is best for us. Your
aim goes far beyond the solving of a particular problem. Ultimately, what
you want for us is our loving union with you.

Show all of us, whole or infirm, how to trust in the love of your *human heart, which reflects your divine love and compassion. I believe that you will not abandon us in the years ahead. I believe that you will not abandon those close to us. Increase our faith. Amen.*

A YOUNG FATHER UNDERGOES OPEN HEART SURGERY

David had started a business selling and repairing computers and printers. It wasn't long before the business was showing a good profit. David was able to keep up his payments on a loan from the bank and have enough left over to meet the needs of his family. Actually, the family income came from both David and his wife Beverly, because she was his partner in the business.

David and Beverly were both in their mid-thirties and had three children, all under the age of twelve. Beverly and David shared the responsibilities of the home as well as of the business. The children were not orphans, though they spent more time with hired teenaged caretakers than with their parents.

The two of them were pursuing the same dream that motivated countless other couples. They anticipated a life of comfort and affluence even during their working years: a fine, expensively furnished house, a small fleet of automobiles which would tell them, their children and their neighbors that they had arrived, the best modern electronic devices for their pleasure, and membership in exclusive clubs. Someday, they would be able to travel abroad whenever they wished and, at home, take their place among the senior social leaders in the community.

Late one evening when the two of them had returned home from the shop, their pursuit of the dream was interrupted when David experienced chest pain. At first he discounted it, believing it was due to stress from his long work week. However, when the pain continued he decided to be safe and visited the emergency room of a nearby hospital. There, an EKG indicated that David had had a small heart attack. The hospital phoned his personal doctor. When he arrived a short time later, he arranged for an angiogram and possible angioplasty on the following morning. David was given medication and sent home. That evening, as he and Beverly sat in the parlor, he said, "I'm too young to have heart trouble."

"I think we have both been pushing too hard," Beverly responded. "Maybe when you're fixed up we ought to take a vacation."

"Who will watch the store?" he asked.

"If you or I are not alive, there won't be anyone to watch the store or our children," she answered.

After David was taken to the catherization lab the next morning, Beverly sat in a surgical waiting area. Her brother and sister were with her to give her support. An hour later, the doctor who had performed the angiogram informed her that David's coronary arteries were severely blocked. Because of the extent of the blockage, a surgeon would immediately begin bypass surgery.

As the hours passed, and no word came from the operating room, Beverly became more and more apprehensive. Morning became early afternoon. Finally a nurse who had been sent as an emissary came to her and told her that the doctor was having difficulty weaning David off the heart-lung machine and starting his heart again. It was evident that the surgeon was preparing Beverly for possible bad news. The nurse explained that a person could be on a heart-lung machine for only a limited number of hours before the blood began to break down. The next hour would be critical.

Beverly began to pray. If David did not recover, she would be alone. What would she do? She pleaded with the Lord, not only for David, but for herself. A half hour later, the same nurse came to tell Beverly that the doctor had restored David's heartbeat and that the operation was a success. A couple of hours later, when her husband was out of recovery and put to bed in the intensive care unit, she was allowed to visit him.

In the days that followed, she spent almost all of her time in the hospital near her husband. When he was out of danger and moved to a regular room, she began a conversation with him telling him about her experience while he was on the operating table. She told him about praying that the Lord would bring him through.

"I haven't prayed much for a long time," she said. "It felt strange to be asking God to spare you when I haven't spared much time for God. I got to thinking too about our lives together. We have a lot that is good going for us. We love one another and we love our children. But we also spend so much time trying to get things that we really don't need. We've had no place for God in our lives. We haven't been to church for a long time. Maybe, when you're better, we should go back to church. I'm sure the priest will be surprised."

As David listened to his wife, he could hear that a message from above had somehow reached her. She had indeed planted a seed. Another month passed before the seed began to sprout. Beverly had already resumed going to Sunday Mass. One Sunday morning, David offered to accompany her. The topic of the gospel and sermon was ideal for David's spiritual need:

"For what will it profit them if they gain the whole world but forfeit their life? Or what will they give in return for their life?" (Mt 16:26).

David reviewed his values and his priorities. He could see the finger of God in his last minute reprieve on the operating table. And he could see the compassionate love of Jesus reaching out to help him in spite of the fact that he had neglected God and the Church. By the time the Mass ended, he decided to rearrange his life to make a place for the Lord. Soon, David and Beverly both found a new spirit in their home. Life was less hectic. The children saw their parents more frequently. They themselves found the peace which comes from a close bond with the heart of Jesus.

～ PRAYER ～

Lord Jesus, you were always concerned about the household of David and Beverly and its needs. You were concerned about their material needs and their children. However, you were much more concerned about the spiritual welfare of all five of them. A dividend of their being able to find time for you in their lives and moderate the intensity of their pursuit of worldly success was a life that is much more meaningful in the long run.

I pray that you may show all the hurried people in this world how to find the time to renew their acquaintance with you, even without the need for a near medical catastrophe. I pray that you may become for them more than an acquaintance—that they may discover you as a friend and a lover who wants an intimate union with them. The life that you offer them is precisely a loving bond with you in this world and the next. You alone can be a "possession" which they cannot lose if they choose to receive your gift of yourself.

Bless their homes with your presence. Their children will learn from them what is most important in life. Their children's lasting success and happiness will depend on what they learn from the example of their parents and their own free choices. In the larger world, what a marvelous place it would be if everyone lived in harmony with you and your will for them! In times of health and prosperity, they would thank you for your gifts. In times of sickness and infirmity, your peace would prevail to give them the support they need.

I thank you for your loving kindness which reaches out, sometimes again and again, to draw all people to yourself so that they might find a life that really matters and which never ends. Amen.

A YOUNG WOMAN HAS A HYSTERECTOMY

Gloria visited her gynecologist to discover the reason for the abnormal bleeding which had begun several weeks earlier. Her mother and an aunt had died of cancer of the uterus. Gloria feared that she had inherited a predisposition to the same disease.

After examining her and studying the results of laboratory tests, the doctor suspected that Gloria might need to have a hysterectomy and decided to do exploratory surgery. She also obtained Gloria's prior permission to perform a hysterectomy if that was necessary. The doctor soon discovered that the removal of Gloria's uterus was necessary. There had indeed been a malignant growth, but it was small and there was no evidence that the cancer had spread to other organs. Gloria had wisely sought medical attention in time.

However, afterward Gloria was devastated. She would never be able to be a mother. From her teen-age years, that had been her main ambition in life. She saw motherhood as her supreme fulfillment as a woman. She had no interest at all in a career outside the home, though she would be willing to work part time to help pay the bills. She was twenty-five, and her husband August, who was an assistant professor of biology, was twenty-eight. They had been trying to have a child for five years, but when Gloria could not get pregnant August underwent fertility tests. When he was found to be fertile, Gloria began considering the use of fertility drugs. Now that option was closed by the operation which had laid waste to her dream.

As she lay in her hospital bed the evening after the hysterectomy, August sat by her side, holding her hand. He concealed his disappointment for her sake. She was grateful that she had a husband who loved her so much that even this blow to his desire for children did not separate him from her. Indeed, his sole concern seemed to be for her welfare and comfort.

After August had returned home, Gloria picked up a Bible by her bedside and opened it. She came upon the 127th Psalm:

Unless the Lord builds the house,
> those who build it labor in vain.
Unless the Lord guards the city,
> the guard keeps watch in vain.
It is in vain that you rise up early
> and go late to rest,
eating the bread of anxious toil;
> for he gives sleep to his beloved.
Sons are indeed a heritage from the Lord,
> the fruit of the womb a reward.
Like arrows in the hand of a warrior
> are the sons of one's youth.
Happy is the man who has
> his quiver full of them.
He shall not be put to shame
> when he speaks with his enemies in the gate.

Gloria looked at a crucifix on the wall and asked, "What is to be my heritage? Where are the sons or daughters of my youth?" She began to weep, not only for herself but also for August. Would he maintain his love for her in the absence of the family he desired? What would happen to their relationship without the bond which comes from caring together for their children? Were they doomed to live always in an empty nest?

It seemed to her that Jesus was looking down at her with compassion and concern. He understood her pain and her perplexity. He had a heart which was thoroughly human. Not only had he endured great personal grief, but he had felt the sorrow in the heart of his own mother and could now feel Gloria's sorrow.

Of course, the crucifix did not speak to her, but while she was gazing at the Lord and weeping, there came to her mind the image of her sister, who was a nun. Theresa too would never have children of her own, and she didn't have a husband to comfort her. Theresa worked with disabled youngsters at a special school. Gloria had long admired her dedication and had envied her joy. Theresa seemed to find more satisfaction in her way of life than most married women whom Gloria had known. Theresa had told her that she could see Jesus in every crippled body and crippled mind. The children in her care completely fulfilled Theresa's maternal nature. Moreover, the children for whom she cared so lovingly adored her.

It was at this point in her dialogue with the crucifix that Gloria began to consider the possibility of adoption. It would not be the same as having her own children. Yet it would not be without its rewards. And it would answer some of the questions she had just asked. Gloria felt sure that August would agree. Moreover, there were children out there who needed parents, just as she and August needed children.

Her faith in Jesus' love was strong. He would be with her and August as they gave the opportunity for a more full life to some otherwise abandoned child, perhaps to more than one. Jesus was asking her to be his loving outreach to children who would otherwise be deprived of parental love. Gloria dried her tears and peacefully fell asleep.

➤ PRAYER ➤

Often what seems at first to be a catastrophe is, in fact, the beginning of an opportunity. When a couple cannot have children of their own, they can reach out to youngsters who otherwise would have no one to care for them. The bonds can become nearly as strong as those which parents share with their own offspring. In addition, they have the satisfaction of knowing that they are fostering a life which might otherwise have led to ruin because of a lack of the love which they could offer.

Lord Jesus, we are all the adopted children of your Father. You are his own Son. Yet the Father sees in us a reflection of yourself and loves us because he loves you so much. On the banks of the Jordan, the Father declared, "This is my Son, the Beloved, with whom I am well pleased" (Mt. 3:17). Much later, you told Mary Magdalene, "But go to my brothers and say to them, 'I am ascending to my Father and your Father, to my God and your God'" (Jn. 20:17b). Each of us, therefore, is a beloved son or daughter, and who can be more so than a little child.

In one way, therefore, you draw parents who cannot have children of their own closer to yourself and your Father for their own benefit. In another way, you enable them to extend your embrace to a child that you dearly love. Thank you for giving them this opportunity, which began in a moment of sorrow. Thank you for drawing joy out of their sorrow. Amen.

Chapter 3: I've Lost Control of My Life

Most people believe they have control of their lives. They are healthy and have more than enough money, and they look forward to many pleasures and excitements and goals day after day. Even the difficulties that do occur in their lives seem solvable and under their mastery. They believe they can see clearly on the open road ahead as they travel rapidly through the journey of this world.

But long ago the prophet Isaiah offered both a philosophic comment about the human condition, and a prediction about God's response to it:

The people who walked in darkness
    have seen a great light;
those who lived in a land of deep darkness—
    on them light has shined (Is. 9:2).

Until our lives are lived in the light that God gives us, we really walk in darkness. Without faith in God we cannot understand the true meaning of our lives. We who believe in Jesus see him as the light that the Father has sent into the world—the light that Isaiah predicted would one day come and drive out the spiritual darkness in our lives. That light is always shining, but we do not always allow it to illumine our lives.

Then something happens which turns our lives upside down. Suddenly our lives seem to have lost all meaning and direction. We come to see only darkness, which has in fact been there all along. The false lights of human accomplishments have all gone out. This is often a moment of despair. And it is precisely at this moment that Jesus can enter in. The illusion of having the world in your pocket has broken down. Suddenly we recognize the limitations of being human and our own vulnerability. We are ready for grace. If we say "yes" to that grace, the light of Christ begins to shine in our minds and in our hearts.

We learn that the One on whom we are entirely dependent is dependable. The heart of Jesus will never fail us. On one occasion, his apostles were in great distress during a storm at sea. The Gospel tells us:

But immediately he spoke to them and said, "Take heart, it is I; do not be afraid." Then he got into the boat with them and the wind ceased. And they were utterly astounded. . . (Mk. 6:50-51).

In our own storms of life, Jesus comes to abide with us to assure us of his saving power and continued care. He asks only that we let go of our conceit and the darkness of self-sufficiency and open our hearts to the compassionate love and power of his heart.

A Construction Worker Loses an Arm

When a crane tipped over in a heavy wind gust, Bruce's left arm was crushed. He was taken from the construction site to a hospital emergency room, where a surgeon assessed the massive nature of the injury. There was only one possible treatment: amputation of what remained of Bruce's arm. When his wife, Ellen, learned about the accident, she rushed to the hospital, arriving after Bruce had been taken into the operating room. She had left their two young children with her mother so she could be with her husband to support him after the surgery. A chaplain came to offer comfort while she waited. Together, they prayed for Bruce and for Ellen and the children.

After a stay in the recovery room, Bruce was taken to the intermediate care unit, where his wife joined him. Because he was still somewhat groggy, she contented herself with simply letting him know that she was there. When he tried to explain the accident and his fears for his family, she listened and told him that she loved him, that they would somehow manage, and that what mattered now was his recovery. Then they could figure out what they were going to do.

Late in the evening, she picked up the children and took them home for the night. While she tucked them into their beds, she prayed in her heart that Jesus would watch over them and protect them during the weeks, months and perhaps years to come, while their father was disabled.

Ironically, the accident had occurred on the Friday before

Labor Day. Bruce realized that he would never again be able to do construction work. His days of manual labor were over. During the Labor Day weekend, he spent much time worrying about his future and the future of his family. He also prayed. He had been raised in a practicing Catholic home but, in his youth and younger adult years, he had drifted away from religious practice. It was only when his oldest daughter was preparing for First Communion that he took another look at the lack of religion in his life. At first, he resumed going to church for his daughter's sake. Then he discovered that his newfound religion was good for his spirits. He felt better about life at home and on the job.

When Labor Day came he ached to be enjoying the holiday at a family picnic and barbecue. Instead, he turned on the TV in his recovery room, using the remote, just as Mass was beginning in the hospital chapel. The priest was celebrating the "Mass for the Blessing of Human Labor." At the Gospel, Bruce heard the words of Jesus:

"Therefore do not worry, saying, 'What will we eat?' or 'What will we drink?' or 'What will we wear?' For it is the Gentiles who strive for all these things; and indeed your heavenly Father knows that you need all these things. But strive first for the kingdom of God and his righteousness, and all these things will be given to you as well. So do not worry about tomorrow, for tomorrow will bring worries of its own. Today's trouble is enough for today" (Mt. 6:31-34).

The priest's message was that one way to lose peace of mind and peace of heart is to become obsessed with getting results. He said, "We can dwell on what may happen tomorrow or next week or next year. Jesus would have us be at peace now, the only moment that actually exists. A little voice deep inside may ask, 'Will he be faithful to me?' Even when we shut out the doubting voice as unworthy of a disciple of Jesus, its echo may persist and trouble our peace. The only help is simply to let go and put everything into the hands of the Lord. Only God sees the whole pattern of our lives. Only God knows the graces that he will give. They will arrive when we need them. In the meantime, God asks for our trust."

As Bruce listened to these words, he thought, "It's easy for you to say. You don't have a family. What are my wife and kids going to do when I can't provide more than a disability check to support them?"

Bruce began to feel sorry for himself as well as for those who depended on him. The feeling offended his male ego. He believed that men did not cry, even in their hearts. But what was he to do? Then he remembered the Serenity Prayer, which was hanging on the wall of his parlor at home:

"God grant me the serenity to accept the things I cannot change,
Courage to change the things I can,
And the wisdom to know the difference."

He realized that he was worrying about something he couldn't change. Today's trouble was that he was without an arm. It was enough for today to deal with the healing of the wound. Jesus was asking him to put his own future as well as his family's future into God's care. When the time was right, Jesus would let him know how God would guide their lives and provide for their needs. There was no way he could foresee that now. The meditation brought him peace for the first time since his accident. Eventually, he was able to bring himself to offer a prayer of acceptance, and to place himself in the loving hands of Jesus.

⤳ PRAYER ⤶

Lord Jesus, from day to day none of us can know what the next day will bring. That is as true for those who are healthy and rich as it is for those who are sick and poor. The only sane way to live is to take our circumstances as they are, make reasonable plans for tomorrow and leave them in your hands. That is also the only holy way to live.

I believe that it is safe to trust you. You never gave us guarantees of miraculous solutions to our problems, but you have given us the promise that you will always be near to us and those we love, in our needs. You can use any circumstance to draw us closer to yourself and, in the end, that is what matters most. Sometimes you expect heroic trust. That was certainly true for Bruce and his family. However, when you expect heroic trust you also give great graces. The first grace is to learn to live a day at a time in your loving care.

Watch over those whose losses are far greater than changes of fortune. The loss of a limb cannot be reversed, but financial security can return. If

they have been neglectful of you, lead them to discover your heartfelt com-
passion for them. If they have been faithful, lead them to a deeper under-
standing of what it means to follow you in your passion, death and res-
urrection. Then whatever happens in their lives they will be able to say:

> *Let all who take refuge in you rejoice;*
> *let them ever sing for joy.*
> *Spread your protection over them,*
> *so that those who love your name may exult in you.*
> *For you bless the righteous, O Lord;*
> *you cover them with favor as with a shield (Ps. 5:11-12).*

Thank you, Lord Jesus, for every grace, in good times and bad. Thank
you for your everlasting love. Amen.

A SINGER HAS CANCER OF THE LARYNX

At the age of eight, Anne had already decided that she wanted
to be a singer. Both of her parents were musicians who played in a
local symphony orchestra. Their home was a house of music. It was
the very life of all of them—her parents, her two older sisters and
herself. One sister had become a fine violist; the other was a
skilled pianist.

Anne liked to sing. Even as a child she received many compli-
ments about her voice when she sang at gatherings of relatives and
in the choir of Calvary Presbyterian Church. In her teen years she

studied with a retired operatic soprano who had had an illustrious career before she decided to leave behind the stress of continuous performances. Anne worked her way up from small parts in a local opera company. One day, she auditioned for a place in an internationally famous opera company and was accepted for a minor role. Over the years, she had become a diva.

The first sign that something was wrong appeared when her voice broke during a performance. The audience booed, and Anne was devastated. However, her spirits fell much further when the doctor who attended members of the company examined her throat and detected a growth on her vocal cords. He sent her to a clinic for a more thorough assessment. The oncologist at the clinic diagnosed a malignancy which would require surgery. He would have to remove not only the growth but nearby tissue as well. Anne's singing career was at an end.

As Anne lay in her bed following the surgery, despair was overwhelming. She could not contemplate life without singing. Indeed, was life even worth living without the ability to sing? She had never considered any other way of expressing her musical soul.

When her parents and older sisters visited her, she could feel their pity. In one way, that consoled her. In another way, it did not. She did not want pity. She wanted to be able to sing. During her time in the hospital and early convalescence at home, Anne continued to brood over her predicament. She lived with her parents and found herself becoming impatient with them when they tried to be helpful. She could see that she was becoming a sour woman.

Anne decided to attend a healing retreat. She did not want to live her life in bitterness. She needed healing in her spirit.

As she meditated in the periods of silence between conferences, it became clearer to her that she had no control over her predicament. She recalled Milton's sonnet on his blindness, where he wrote: "They also serve who only stand and wait." As a blind poet, he was seriously impaired in the one activity that gave him creative pleasure, but Milton's situation was different from her own. He had a daughter to whom he could dictate his poetry. Beethoven too, in his deafness, had no trouble hearing his Ninth Symphony in his head. Anne could not dictate her singing and did not want to hear it only in her head.

During one silent period she found herself staring at a picture of Jesus in her room. It was the familiar scene in the Garden of Gethsemane. She had not thought much about that scene before, but now she realized that at that moment Jesus had no control of his life. He would soon be taken captive. He would be subject to ridicule and apparent failure in regard to everything important to him. Surely, her situation was not worse than his. She also realized that the heart of Jesus would understand her feelings and be supportive of her as she struggled to make a new life for herself. She would have to deal with more treatment, some risk of a recurrence of cancer, and the finding of a new outlet for her creative temperament.

There is perhaps nothing more difficult than surrendering something which is good and true and beautiful. It can be hard to give up a vice or a destructive addiction. It is far harder to give up a glory of the human spirit which flows from a divine quality within us. Anne knew that her voice had glorified God and had proclaimed the beauty of the human soul that God had given her. Now, she would have to search for a new way to fulfill God's gift. At the moment, Anne did not know what that might be, but she resolved to walk with Jesus day by day, trusting that he would take care of her.

When Anne returned home after the retreat, she began to plan how she might use her knowledge to help others appreciate music. For several years, she had occasionally given music appreciation sessions among underprivileged children in a poorer section of town. She resolved now to make this a regular part of her life. She also resolved to begin, even at her relatively advanced age, to learn how to play the violin. Her violinist sister could help her until Anne could find a professional teacher of violin.

Anne had lost her voice, but she had not lost something far more precious, namely, *the will to be and to do what she believed Jesus would have her be and do*, and to do it as well as she could. She sensed that Jesus approved of her decision not to simply die within herself. He wanted her to be fully alive in a new way, and he would guide her into a future which had once again become bright.

⤙ P R A Y E R ⤚

Lord Jesus, you were stripped of everything during the course of your passion. The taking away of your clothing was only a symbol of the deep-

er deprivation which you suffered on Calvary. Yet, through your loss, we have been greatly enriched. You told us that, in some way, we must all die to ourselves so that we may come to life. We need to lose in order to gain the opportunities which can bring us closer to you and enable us to help others to find fulfillment. The fruit of Anne's sacrifice will be opportunities for children who would not otherwise have had her for their teacher.

In this way, Lord Jesus, you arranged that one voice would become many voices which praise you, for you are the giver of every good gift. Thank you for inspiring those who lose their personal dream to adopt your dream for what they can become. Thank you for giving fulfillment to them and to many others through them.

Graciously grant us all the wisdom to know how to use your gifts. May we praise you with the beauty of the song which comes from our hearts. May we proclaim you, not only in voices which may be impaired, but by our loving concern for others in need. That song will always reach the hearts of those whom you would move to know and love you. Amen.

A BUSINESS EXECUTIVE WITH A BROKEN NECK

At age 40, Steve was quite young to be the CEO of a billion dollar corporation. As CEO he was used to being in charge. The junior executives in his company made great efforts to please him. He vastly enjoyed the prerogatives of power: the large corner office, his exclusive place in the parking garage, and deference at every turn.

Steve carried over his will to control into his household. His wife Genevieve and their two teenaged sons had learned not to contradict him. His temper flared if they wanted to discuss what he had already decided. When he would go fishing for a weekend with a friend who was also an executive, one boy might say to the other, "Thank God, the 800 pound gorilla is gone for a few days."

It was while coming back from a fishing trip that Steve had his accident. He was the driver and, therefore, had limited himself to a couple of beers before leaving the cabin. Still, his reflexes were not capable of handling the car when its right wheels ran on to a soft shoulder while he was traveling at a high speed. In seconds the car was headed down an embankment aiming directly at a low stump at the edge of a farmer's field. When the car hit the stump, it went into a forward flip and landed on its roof. Both Steve and his companion were wearing their seat belts. The friend sustained only bruises and scrapes. Steve's head was pounded by the ceiling of the car. Immediately, he could feel that something was wrong with his neck.

As soon as the shock had begun to subside, his friend made a call using a cellular phone and, in ten minutes, a husky paramedic who was careful not to move his head was lifting Steve out of the car. In a local hospital, Steve was diagnosed as having a fracture of the second cervical vertebra. In lay terms, he had a broken neck. Steve was placed on his back in a bed, and a pulley at the head of the bed applied traction on his neck. He was not allowed to move from lying on his back.

The nurse instructed him to use the call button to summon her for any need which might arise. It would be better for him not to try to do anything for himself. She then proceeded to bathe him, with the loving care a mother might show to her infant son. Steve felt that his dignity was compromised by his dependence on her. A greater indignity occurred later when he had to summon a nurse's aide to help him use a bedpan. Steve was angry and spoke to the aide in a tone which clearly told her that she was merely tolerated.

Steve's attitude and mood did not improve during his first few weeks in traction. When the chaplain visited him and asked him if he wanted a Bible, Steve told him that he had long since gotten that religious stuff out of his life. He did not need God. He didn't need the Methodist faith in which he had been raised. He didn't need anyone else for that matter. Other people needed him. The chaplain could not break through his shell.

Steve rightly perceived that he is a person with dignity. The book of Genesis tells us:

> Then God said, "Let us make humankind in our image, according to our likeness; and let them have dominion over the fish of the sea, and over the birds of the air, and over the cattle, and over all the wild animals of the earth, and over every creeping thing that creeps upon the earth." So God created humankind in his image, in the image of God he created them; male and female he created them (Gen. 1:26-27).

Steve's mistake was that he enjoyed having virtually total dominion over other people. He didn't think that a CEO needed to be sensitive to the feelings of subordinates. Yet, from God's point of view, we were created to respect one another's dignity.

Steve's broken neck did not heal rapidly. As weeks turned into months, the humiliation of his hospital bed gradually became for him a school of humility. The breakthrough began when a nurse who had had enough of him said, "Why does a grown man like you have to act like a baby?" When she left the room, Steve thought about her words and, in a moment of insight, saw that what she said was true. He really did need her services. Indeed, he needed the services of many people as he lay helpless in his bed.

None of us can avoid humiliation. The Son of God, whose dignity was divine, was himself profoundly humiliated in his passion and death on the cross. Through his humiliation Jesus came to his resurrection. Humiliation is often a teacher of humility to bring us closer to Jesus and eternal life. He once said:

"I thank you, Father, Lord of heaven and earth, because you have hidden these things from the wise and the intelligent and have revealed them to infants; yes, Father, for such was your gracious will. All things have been handed over to me by my Father; and no one knows the Son except the Father, and no one knows the Father except the Son and anyone to whom the Son chooses to reveal him.

"Come to me, all you that are weary and are carrying heavy burdens, and I will give you rest. Take my yoke upon you, and learn from me; for I am gentle and humble in heart, and you will find rest for your souls. For my yoke is easy, and my burden is light" (Mt. 11:25-30).

The hospital where Steve was recovering was a Catholic hospital. There was a crucifix high on the wall where he would easily see it even while in traction. In another moment of insight, Steve was struck by the fact that the figure on the cross was even more restrained than he was. That was all the enlightenment Steve received that day. Over the next month, however, Steve had many other moments of reflection on the One who hung on the cross. With some encouragement from the chaplain, he came to see the love with which Jesus had offered himself for him. Jesus had freely chosen to be nailed to a cross so that Steve could be freed from his pride as he lay fixed to his bed.

When Steve was finally able to leave the hospital wearing a brace, He was a very different person from the one who entered it on a gurney. He had come in as an 800 pound gorilla and he left as a man who had learned what really mattered in life. He had rediscovered Jesus and found the peace which comes from humility. It would take Steve a while to unlearn old habits and acquire new ways of behaving. Nevertheless, a dividend of his change of heart was that his family and employees would finally have deliverance from his outbursts of anger.

❧ PRAYER ☙

Lord Jesus, how often those of us who think we are in control of our lives suddenly discover that we are no longer in control. We may be treated like infants, cared for by loving people who do everything for us. Our affliction has made us powerless and we feel shamed by the kindness of our nurses. How can they not look down on us? We begin to look down on ourselves. What is our worth now that we lie helpless in our beds?

Steve, in particular, always tried to take care of himself, and not only himself but his family as well. He was a good provider. That part pleased you, Lord Jesus. What displeased you was his extreme care to arrange his life so that he was always in control. Until his accident, he thought that he had been successful, but that was only an illusion. You knew that he needed to learn that none of us ever have the kind of control we think we have. If it were otherwise, Steve would not have found himself lying helpless in his bed, cared for by others and ashamed of himself. Then, when he looked at you hanging on the cross, he saw your side pierced for him and a helplessness far beyond his own. He began to realize how much you loved him.

He realized too that your love and care for his soul was not demeaning. You know who each of us really is in the eyes of your Father. No one and nothing can take away our essential worth. Your Father has made us a reflection of the divine. You have made us your adopted brothers and sisters. As members of the family of your Father, our essential worth far exceeds all earthly power and glory.

The greatness of our souls cannot come from our unaided efforts. I believe that you would have all of us come to a deeper understanding of where our true worth lies. From our present affliction we can discover the wisdom that caused you to break out in a hymn of praise to your Father for revealing the truth to little ones.

Teach us to be willing to do whatever we need to do to cooperate with those who care for us in our needs. Then, lead us to abandon ourselves entirely into your care, to be led closer to you in your humiliation on the cross and closer to your glory in heaven. I pray for patience for all who suffer the humiliations of infirmity, and for the wisdom which is above all worldly wisdom. Amen.

Chapter 4: Where Are My Golden Years?

When I was a seminarian, occasionally, like every other seminarian and college student, there were times when I had little enthusiasm for studying. One afternoon, to entertain myself, I opened the book of Genesis and played with the numbers given in chapter five for the ages of the descendants of Adam. The Hebrew Scriptures tell us that Noah's grandfather, Methuselah, lived 969 years. Using the years of births and begettings, I calculated that Methuselah died in the year of the Flood. Evidently, in his ripe old age, he would not have been able to take the strain of living in the ark.

Today we call old age the "golden years." Although we've given this time of life a catchy name to make it more appealing, there is nothing new about this state of being. The "golden years" are well described in the book of Ecclesiastes:

> Remember your creator in the days of your youth, before the days of trouble come, and years draw near when you will say, "I have no pleasure in them"; before the sun and the light and the moon and the stars are darkened and the clouds return with the rain; in the day when the guards of the house tremble, and the strong men are bent, and the women who grind cease working because they are few, and those who look through the windows see dimly; when the doors on the street are shut, and

the sound of the grinding is low, and one rises up at the sound of a bird, and all the daughters of song are brought low; when one is afraid of heights, and terrors are in the road; the almond tree blossoms, the grasshopper drags itself along and desire fails; because all must go to their eternal home, and the mourners will go about the streets; before the silver cord is snapped, and the golden bowl is broken, and the pitcher is broken at the fountain, and the wheel broken at the cistern, and the dust returns to the earth as it was, and the breath returns to God who gave it. Vanity of vanities, says the Teacher; all is vanity (Eccl. 12:1-8).

This metaphor for what happens when sight and hearing fail, when one is toothless and weak, deprived of all pleasures of the flesh and at risk of broken bones if one should fall, is more and more the experience of modern people. We live much longer than people generally did when this scripture was written. However, there are other ways to lose one's "golden years," and they can be quite distressing. Jesus loves those who are so afflicted just as much, if not more, than when they were in full health. He has a preference for those who are in greater need of his love.

A DIABETIC LOSES HER SIGHT

During the forty-five years Virginia had worked at the Elson Construction Company as a secretary, she had looked forward to the day when she and her husband Joe could both retire and begin to enjoy financial security and freedom from a work schedule. Their wish list of things to do included regular trips to see their six children and thirteen grandchildren located from one coast to the other, tours in Europe, Alaska and the Caribbean, and occasional fun and games in Las Vegas. She had been working as a secretary since she was nineteen. Now, just short of sixty-five, she found herself not on a tour boat but in a clinic receiving a bad report from her eye doctor.

Her diabetes had been largely under control throughout her working life. Then Virginia gradually began to lose her sight. Her doctor informed her that she would soon become blind, and that there was nothing medical science could do to prevent that outcome. Joe had taken her to the clinic. When they returned home, he prepared a lunch for them both and then went to their bedroom to rest. His early afternoon nap had become a daily routine ever since he retired from his work as a carpenter during the previous year.

Virginia sat in the parlor, musing over their life together. They had met soon after she began work at the construction company. The twenty-year-old Joe was helping his father on one of the jobs contracted by the company. When he walked into the office one day, Virginia was immediately attracted to him. She could see in his eyes that he was attracted to her. Thus began a courtship which led to marriage a year later. They had always enjoyed one another's company. Their marriage was unusual in that serious arguments were quite rare. That is one of the reasons they anticipated a happy retirement in their later years. Then Virginia's thoughts turned back to her blindness.

"What has become of our golden years?" Virginia wondered. "This will be as hard on Joe as it is on me. Will his retirement now mean taking care of me? I will try not to be a burden on him."

Fortunately for both of them, Virginia and Joe had never let their seeking of security interfere with their regular worship of God. They had raised their children in the faith they had received from their own parents. They had long ago taken to heart Jesus' message in the Gospel of Luke:

> Then he told them a parable: "The land of a rich man produced abundantly. And he thought to himself, 'What should I do, for I have no place to store my crops?' Then he said, 'I will do this: I will pull down my barns and build larger ones, and there I will store all my grain and my goods. And I will say to my soul, 'Soul, you have ample goods laid up for many years; relax, eat, drink, be merry.' But God said to him, 'You fool! This very night your life is being demanded of you. And the things you have prepared, whose will they be?' So it is with those who store up treasures for themselves but are not rich toward God" (Lk. 12:16-21).

Material well-being had never been the center of their lives. They had always taken much more satisfaction in spiritual values, including their love and fidelity toward one another, a good relationship with their children and neighbors, and living with integrity in a world where integrity is often sacrificed to expediency. They had always tried to live in accord with their consciences and to accept the will of God in the passing trials of life.

Nevertheless, having to let go of their innocent dreams for a happy old age was a painful shock for Virginia, and she knew that it was a painful shock for Joe, though he would never say so. All that would sustain them would be their belief that the heart of Jesus was preparing a happy eternity for them together. Virginia was grateful for the consolation of their faith in Jesus. Virginia prayed that they might even now, in spite of her infirmity, have some consolation together in this world. She found the place in her bedside Bible where the psalmist prays:

> Bless the Lord, O my soul,
>> and all that is within me,
>> bless his holy name.
>
> Bless the Lord, O my soul,
>> and do not forget all his benefits—
>
> who forgives all your iniquity,
>> who heals all your diseases,
>
> who redeems your life from the Pit,
>> who crowns you with steadfast love and mercy,
>
> who satisfies you with good as long as you live
>> so that your youth is renewed like the eagle's (Ps 103:1-5).

Somehow, Virginia was convinced, Jesus' concern for them would make a way to happiness in their old age, though of a different kind than they had planned. Their youthful love, which had never faded but had rather grown, would give them much more than the relaxation and entertainment of their dreams. When Joe awakened, she would share these thoughts with him, as she shared everything else. Virginia knew in her heart that he would agree with her and that what had happened to her was a new beginning, not an ending. Even on that day of bad news, she was able to find peace in the love of the heart of Jesus for her and Joe. His love had entered not only into each of them but into their relationship. Joe cherished her as much as she cherished him. In Jesus' care, what did they have to fear?

⤙ PRAYER ⤚

Lord Jesus, the only blindness which can have a lasting effect on our happiness is that which is unable to see the fulfillment which you have prepared for those who trust you and love you. We can become so preoccupied with our present distress and our fears for the future that we can forget your mercy in the past and your pledge to those who simply abandon themselves to your love.

In your ministry in ancient Israel, you often restored the sight of people who were blind. The Gospel of Mark tells us that you had compassion on a blind beggar:

> *Then Jesus said to him, "What do you want me to do for you?" The blind man said to him, "My teacher, let me see again." Jesus said to him, "Go, your faith had made you well." Immediately he regained his sight and followed him on the way (Mk 10:51-52).*

Surely, Jesus, you wanted to relieve his earthly distress, but far more importantly you wanted to give him entry into the fellowship of those who were close to you. He became able to follow you up the road. In these miracles, you proved your mission as the One who had been sent by the Father. Even then you were much more concerned with spiritual blindness than with that which is physical.

A person who is physically blind may very well see spiritual truth more clearly because abandonment to the love of Jesus has prepared the way for a better understanding of the heart of the Lord. That does not make physical blindness something to be desired, but it does offer hope of a benefit which many people with perfect vision do not receive because they lack faith in Jesus and his compassionate love. In the end, those who believe in him and follow his way will have the vision which is greater than all others. They will see God.

Lord Jesus, I pray for the people who must live in earthly darkness. Enlighten their minds and fill their hearts with confidence in you so that they may find peace in your love. Enlighten and inspire me too so that I may be able to follow you on the way that you have chosen for me. Amen.

A Stroke Victim Recovers in a Rehab Unit

In midafternoon, the rehabilitation hospital was especially quiet. Most of the residents were napping and the staff had few cares to attend to before four o'clock. Howard, no longer confined to bed, was sitting in a wheelchair. He had regained some power over his left leg, though the doctors expected that he would recover only enough to walk with a cane.

Two months earlier, he and Marian had been planning to go to the beach for a summer vacation. It would be the last time the two of them would need to set aside a couple of weeks in the summer for a stay at the beach. Next year, when both of them retired from their jobs at the bank, they would buy a condominium in Florida and enjoy the beach whenever they chose.

They had worked hard all their lives for that day. Somehow they had managed to raise five children, meeting all their needs on their double salary. For most of their married lives, they had both faithfully put in forty-hour weeks on the job, reserving most of their evenings to be with their children while they were still small. They enjoyed their work, but they would be quite pleased when they could let go of every schedule and simply relax. Then the stroke had occurred.

In the silence of his room, Howard felt himself slipping into self-pity. A tear rolled down his cheek. He didn't want to feel self-pity. It demeaned him. He fought against the feeling. He would fight his disability and get as much freedom of movement as he could. The engine of anger prepared him for the physical therapy session which would begin in about an hour.

During the following months, Howard progressed to the point where he could shuffle along with someone holding him. Then the day came when he could stand and move along slowly with a walker. He made his first long trip to the chapel of the rehabilitation hospital. It was an interfaith chapel and did not have the particular symbols of any religion. It was, however, designed to foster meditation. There, sitting in a chair with his walker by his side, he looked at a small picture of Jesus which Marian had brought for him. It displayed Jesus on the cross and the words: "Lord Jesus, Son of God, have mercy on me, a sinner."

Looking at the picture led Howard to review his life and his goals. He realized in an abstract way that he must be a sinner, because, with the exception of Jesus and Mary, all human beings are sinners. However, he didn't see his life as a sordid succession of sins. Faults, yes; major sins, no. He had always been faithful to Marian. He had taken care of his children alongside Marian. He had been an honest banker and in his personal financial affairs. He wasn't a drunk or a user of drugs, destroying himself and those around him. He had been involved in community affairs, taking his place as a citizen. As a member of his lodge, he had participated in programs designed to help the unfortunate. Yet, somehow, perhaps he had sinned because his religious faith insisted that we were all sinners.

Howard then began to look at his life from another direction. He had depended entirely on himself to reach his goals, including a happy retirement in his old age. There certainly was nothing wrong with wanting to enjoy the golden years with Marian by his side. It was obvious, however, that his goals had assumed circumstances that might not exist when he and Marian were old. There had to be another measure of a successful life.

Contemplating the picture, Howard came to see that the only purpose that really matters in life is to be and do what the Lord would have him be and do, and to fulfill the will of the Lord precisely because it is the will of the Lord. What he had done was good, but it lacked the *why* that only a lively faith can provide. Only faith in Jesus could give his life ultimate meaning, and Jesus could do that in any circumstance. He saw that even when doing good, he had not focused on his relationship with the Lord. Even in his concern for the disadvantaged, he ought to have seen Jesus in them. In spite of the fact that he and Marian attended church regularly, his religion had been superficial. God was more of a social ornament than a reason for his behavior.

His thoughts turned to Marian, who had given him the picture. For the first time, he understood the difference in their religious attitudes. He had always recognized that difference, but had ascribed it to the differing temperaments of men and women. Now, he saw that the reason was much deeper. He was sure that Marian would adjust to the change in their plans because of her faith in Jesus. Now, he could too.

With that thought, he began to accept his disability and come to peace with it. He put himself into the care of the one who was showing him to himself with compassionate love. He softly uttered the words: "Lord Jesus, Son of God, have mercy on me, a sinner."

⤙ P R A Y E R ⤚

Lord Jesus, on one occasion you gave us the parable of the Pharisee and the tax collector:

"Two men went up to the temple to pray, one a Pharisee and the other a tax collector. The Pharisee, standing by himself, was praying thus, 'God, I thank you that I am not like other people: thieves, rogues, adulterers, or even like this tax collector. I fast twice a week; I give a tenth of all my income.' But the tax collector, standing far off, would not even look up to heaven, but was beating his breast and saying, 'God, be merciful to me, a sinner!' I tell you, this man went down to his home justified rather than the other; for all who exalt themselves will be humbled, but all who humble themselves will be exalted" (Lk 18:10-14).

It may well have been true that the Pharisee was faithful to your law in many regards. Yet he lacked the one thing that you considered most important. Though he thanked God that he was not like the tax collector, he failed to recognize that all true goodness comes from divine grace. It was his self-righteousness which was a barrier to his justification.

Howard needed to learn that only you could give a true and lasting worth to his life. In addition, he had to discover that no self-made person can be sure of his or her future. The foundation of a life with meaning had to be the humility to place everything, both himself and his plans, into your hands.

Thank you, Lord Jesus, for the graces which you give to people who, like Howard, need to begin to see what is really important for them, and who is the giver. Enlighten us all so that we may seek our justification from your mercy. Then the good that we do will be good indeed. Amen.

AN OLD NUN'S REFLECTIONS IN A CONVENT INFIRMARY

Sister Agnes sat in her wheelchair in the solarium of the infirmary which had become her home a week earlier. She realized that, ironically, she was one of the lucky ones. Her order, the Sisters of Divine Compassion, had long ago foreseen the day when most of the members would be unable to work and in need of special care. The order had established a trust which guaranteed good medical care and comfortable surroundings for old and infirm sisters. Many sisters in other orders were not so fortunate. They received little more than minimum care in surroundings which were much less pleasant than the solarium in which Sister Agnes reflected on her new way of life.

In the warmth of the summer sun coming through the large windows, she began to doze. She dreamt that she was once more in the classroom in which she had spent fifty years teaching the earliest grades in St. Sabina's Parochial School. Sister Agnes had dearly loved her work, and her children had loved her, expressing their love in many ways. In the midst of this idyll, the sound of a voice from the hallway behind her awakened her abruptly. After a moment, she continued to review her story. It was a very sad day for her when she finally had to let go of her flock and return to the motherhouse to do little more than tend the front desk and answer the phone. Finally, even that had been too much for her failing health. Osteoporosis, arthritis and a weakening heart had taken over her life. Now all she could do was dream about the past.

For a moment, she began to feel sorry for herself, but that

passed quickly. She had never been a woman who complained about the ordinary troubles of life. She had been a cheerful realist in her teaching style and in her relationship with the Lord. She never doubted that kids will be kids. She knew full well that the Lord's trusted servants become old and infirm. She had seen that happen to many others. Now it was her turn.

Looking back over the years when she had visited the infirmary to comfort sisters much older than herself, she knew that not every sister was ready to grow old gracefully. Sister Bernice had never been able to accept the fact that she was no longer mother superior. Every change introduced by the current superior brought bitter criticism to her lips. Sister Agnes suspected that Sister Bernice needed to be angry in order to feel alive. In every other way, she was nearly dead. Sister Martha never became angry. In fact, during her entire sixty years as a Sister of Divine Compassion no one had ever seen her become angry. In her extreme old age, she simply withdrew into herself.

Sister Agnes resolved that she would not let herself follow either path. She had always trusted in the love of the heart of Jesus for her and her children. Now that she was in her golden years she intended to continue to trust in Jesus' love and care for her. One of her favorite Scripture verses was the passage from Jeremiah:

I have loved you with an everlasting love;
therefore I have continued my faithfulness to you (Jer. 31:3).

On the day Sister Agnes had made her religious vows, she was fully aware that she was entering into a covenant with the Lord, like the people of ancient Israel and like the covenant of Jesus' Church with himself. Hers was, to be sure, only a little covenant. Yet it was a share in the great covenant which Jesus had confirmed in his passion, death and resurrection. He had given himself entirely for her and to her. At the moment of pronouncing her vows, she gave herself entirely to him. Her fifty years in the classroom with Jesus' little ones was her way of giving herself for him. She knew that only Jesus could give the grace to make that possible. She could be no more than an instrument of his love. She had been just that with all her heart and soul.

Sister Agnes did not fall into the trap of thinking that she deserved Jesus' faithfulness. If she had done any good in her life, that too was his work. She simply trusted that Jesus would keep his word to her when he had called her to himself in a special way on the day of her vows.

Osteoporosis, arthritis and a failing heart could not deprive her of the joy which she felt when she contemplated the love of Jesus for her. Sitting in the solarium, it seemed to her that it was Jesus' affection for her which was warming her. If only she could pass that feeling along to others who fretted or ran away into themselves in this place!

Meanwhile she would pray for them and try to cheer them up when she met them in the hallways. She resolved that she would always smile even when she encountered the most sour of her sisters. There were others like herself; she would not be alone in this endeavor. Sister Hilary, for example, always had a joke to bring a smile to a face that had nearly forgotten how to smile. It was easy for Sister Agnes to smile at Sister Hilary. It was considerably more difficult to smile at Sister Bernice. Undoubtedly, Sister Bernice needed a smile more.

Sister Agnes was deeply grateful for having been called to be a nun. Now, at the end of her days, she could say with the psalmist:

> The Lord is my chosen portion and my cup;
>> you hold my lot.
> The boundary lines have fallen for me in pleasant places;
>> I have a goodly heritage.
> I bless the Lord who gives me counsel;
>> in the night also my heart instructs me.
> I keep the Lord always before me;
>> because he is at my right hand, I shall not be moved
>> (Ps. 16:5-8).

⤙ PRAYER ⤚

Lord Jesus, King David had been a vigorous young man when you chose him to lead your people. No enemy could defeat him. He foresaw and achieved glory for his kingdom. His power was absolute and he accomplished whatever he set out to do.

In the end, however, it was said of him:

King David was old and advanced in years; and although they covered him with clothes, he could not get warm (1 Kings 1:1).

In the 71st Psalm, a servant of the Lord cries out at the end of his life:

> *Do not cast me off in the time of old age;*
> *do not forsake me when my strength is spent (Ps. 71:9).*

In my own youth, I was a dreamer. I dreamt of what I might accomplish using my talents and had no doubt that I would succeed. At times, I have had success and rejoiced in it. I rarely thought farther ahead than the next challenge. Life was exciting because it was challenging. However, the years have tempered my early enthusiasm. They have also taught me that I am mortal.

I call on you now, Lord Jesus, to be near me and others like myself who are entering old age. We have no refuge except your love. Our bodies are failing, but our spirits remain alive. We appreciate how fragile some of our dreams have been. Yet you have not abandoned us. You have patiently shown us a better way to find true success in our lives.

I believe you would not have us waste our energies regretting that it took us so long to learn our dependence on you. After all, you have given each of us a lifetime to learn that lesson. You waited and acted within our minds and hearts when the hour for our enlightenment finally arrived. If we strive to be and do what you would have us be and do, no infirmity can separate us from you or from reaching the only goal that matters in the end, union with you in this world and the next.

Thank you, Lord Jesus, for encouraging us by our faith in you. Thank you for promising that everyone who believes in you and is faithful to you will arrive safely in paradise. Thank you for your continued care of us *throughout all our lives—from the vigor of youth to this time when our strength is spent. By your grace, our spirits are not crushed. Amen.*

CHAPTER 5: MY FUTURE IS BLEAK

The Israelites endured many grievous troubles at the hands of their enemies during the days of Assyrian and Babylonian captivity in the sixth and seventh centuries before the coming of Jesus. When they were allowed by Cyrus, king of Persia, who had conquered the Babylonians, to return to their own land in 538 B.C., it was a time for consolation and encouragement.

Isaiah prophesied these words of comfort to the Jews who were returning to Judea and Jerusalem from Babylon:

> He will feed his flock like a shepherd;
> > he will gather the lambs in his arms,
> and carry them in his bosom,
> > and gently lead the mother sheep...
> those who wait for the Lord shall renew their strength,
> > they shall mount up with wings like eagles,
> they shall run and not be weary,
> > they shall walk and not faint (Is. 40:11,31).

This passage, and other prophecies as well, were words of comfort and hope that God would restore his people.

Jesus, too, knows that we need divine assurance, particularly when we suffer from a chronic illness or infirmity, which can enslave our spirits as well as our minds and bodies. Many of the words he spoke to all who follow him have special meaning for those whose future seems to them so bleak. One favorite saying is in Matthew 11:28:

> "Come to me, all you that are weary and are carrying heavy burdens, and I will give you rest."

Every day is a time of hope because each day we see the coming of Jesus into our lives. He invites us to begin our day by opening our hearts to him. He wants us to acknowledge our need for him and to be willing to turn our lives over into his care. Then Jesus enables us, who are earth-bound and suffering, to rise above ourselves, to soar on eagles' wings. He does this for quite ordinary people.

The only talent we need is to believe in him and follow him. Jesus does indeed expect faith and, joined to our faith, the humility to allow him to lead us. Jesus has revealed himself as a compassionate heart. He did this in deed as well as word during his ministry in ancient Israel, and he still gives rest to all in need who are willing to trust him. Though he is God, he is not ashamed of being human. Though we are only human, he enables us to become more like God in our daily life.

A MAN WITH BIPOLAR DISORDER IS AGAIN HOSPITALIZED

When he was a teenager, Gerald did not understand his mood

swings. There were days when a gloomy mood would descend on him, without any obvious reason for the gloom. Occasionally, he became so active that his parents wondered whether he was using some street drug. However, they could find no evidence of this. One evening when he was sitting in the parlor with his father, Gerald asked him what was happening to him. His father didn't know what to say. Between themselves, both parents ascribed Gerald's mood swings to the usual ups and downs of growing up through the critical years of adolescence. They were nonplussed when the pattern continued past his teen years.

He was twenty-four when he first attempted suicide during a particularly severe bout of depression. He had secluded himself in his bedroom and swallowed an entire bottle of sleeping pills. When he didn't appear for the evening meal, his mother went to his room and found her son lying unconscious on his bed. Paramedics picked him up and took him to a local hospital, where his stomach was pumped out and he was placed in a special room to recover while under suicide observation. A day and a half later, he was transferred to the psychiatric unit of the same hospital. It was then that he was diagnosed as having a serious mental illness. A combination of profound depression and occasional manic elation and hyperactivity indicated that he suffered from bipolar disorder (a condition of excessive mood swings from manic to depressive states).

Gerald accepted the diagnosis. After he left the hospital, he was more faithful in using the prescribed medications than many other persons with this disorder. His life at home with his parents was relatively normal, and he generally functioned quite well on the job as a junior executive.

Still, in spite of his care during the past ten years, he had several recurrences of deep depression or manic agitation that required his return to the hospital for adjustment of his medication. That pattern was likely to continue. These episodes were possibly dangerous and certainly disruptive of his family life and work during the intervals when they occurred. His future looked bleak.

Over the years, Gerald turned to religion to find a way out of his difficulties. He joined an interfaith charismatic group which prayed over him. Thus far, he had not been delivered from his affliction in a lasting way. Nevertheless, he believed in the Lord. In the privacy of his room, Gerald found Bible accounts of how Jesus cured people who were suffering from illnesses in some ways similar to his own. For example, he read in the Gospel of Matthew:

When they came to the crowd, a man came to him, knelt before him, and said, "Lord, have mercy on my son, for he is an epileptic and he suffers terribly; he often falls into the fire and often into the water. And I brought him to your disciples, but they could not cure him." Jesus answered, "You faithless and perverse generation, how much longer must I put up with you? Bring him here to me." And Jesus rebuked the demon, and it came out of him, and the boy was cured instantly. Then the disciples came to Jesus privately and said, "Why could we not cast it out?" He said to them, "Because of your little faith. For truly I tell you, if you have faith the size of a mustard seed, you will say to this mountain, 'Move from here to there,' and it will move; and nothing will be impossible for you" (Mt. 17:14-21).

Evil spirits can indeed afflict human beings. However, at the time of the Gospel scene people believed that epilepsy and mental disorders were always caused by demons. Sometimes, even today, those who suffer may believe this. Gerald rightly understood that the cause of his illness was chemical rather than spiritual. To his way of thinking, a physical problem would be easier for Jesus to heal. He believed that he trusted Jesus. Why then was he not cured?

When he turned to the writings of Paul, where Paul writes of seeing special revelations from God, he found a passage which gave him a clue to the answer. Paul said that he had "a thorn in the flesh." Although he did not say what it was, it could well have been a physical problem. He writes:

To keep me from being too elated, a thorn was given me in the flesh, a messenger of Satan to torment me. Three times I appealed to the Lord about this, that it would leave me, but he said to me, "My grace is sufficient for you, for power is made perfect in weakness." So, I will boast all the more gladly of my weaknesses, so that the power of Christ may dwell in me. Therefore I am content with weaknesses, insults, hardships, persecutions, and calamities for the sake of Christ; for whenever I am weak, then I am strong (2 Cor. 12:7-10).

Gerald had not had Paul's extraordinary revelations. He had, however, received the grace of deep faith and love of Jesus. His powerlessness over his illness tempered any conceit he might have had over these gifts. After reading Paul's words, Gerald realized that his illness did not separate him from Jesus. That is what mattered most in his life. Sick or well, the power of Christ dwelt in him. He was able to turn his mind and heart toward the Lord, thank him for his gifts and put his future in Jesus' hands.

ᕳ PRAYER ᕱ

You alone, Lord Jesus, know the divine reasons why we who believe in you sometimes suffer greatly in this world. Surely, you are concerned about our suffering. However, you are more concerned about our salvation. Salvation is a work of divine power. Thus, each of us can say with St. Paul, "…whenever I am weak, then I am strong."

Mental illnesses can be particularly distressing to those who believe in you, Lord. The sadness of those who are profoundly depressed, the anxieties of those whose lives are controlled by fear, the delusions of those who are psychotic—all of these can paint a picture of a future that is bleak. In their distress, some of them find you. You said: "I am the way, and the truth, and the life" (Jn. 14:6).

Those who wander in the darkness or amidst perils can find their way when you are with them. Their faith in your presence is an encouragement and a balm for their fears. Your truth sustains them even when they are tormented by delusions.

To be sure, not everyone finds you, but those who do begin to be able

to live again even in the presence of their illnesses. I have known griev-
ously deluded people who learned to listen to you rather than their "voices" when you spoke to them through the scripture or a kindly counselor. I
have known people so sad that only their confidence in your love gave
them a reason to live. I have known anxious souls who eventually found
deliverance when they were able to give their burdens over to you. In
all these instances, you were with them from the beginning of their trials,
gradually leading them to abandon themselves entirely into the
care of your loving heart. In heaven, there will be many who will
praise you because of your tender care for them in this world in their
hours of darkness.

I praise you now and thank you for the mercies you have shown to
the troubled souls to whom you have sent me as a minister of your love.
I thank you for their faith and their courage. Abide with me and with
them, as we follow your lead until we come to the place where there are
no troubles of mind or spirit. Amen.

A Young Alcoholic Woman Has Cut Her Wrist

At age twenty-seven, Sandra had been drinking heavily and
using other drugs since she was in her mid-teens. After dropping
out of high school, she had supported herself as a waitress.
Although she had been attractive as a teenaged girl, her beauty had
begun to fade as a result of her abuse of alcohol and other drugs.
Along the way, she had acquired a live-in boyfriend, Hank, who
worked on the docks as a stevedore. She was drawn to Hank not

only because he was handsome and a great lover, but because he drank and used other drugs in the same way she did. When she was twenty she had her first abortion. She couldn't see herself taking care of a baby and maintaining the life style to which her boyfriend and she had become accustomed.

One day Hank disappeared. Sandra had known for a few weeks that he was fond of another woman who was a co-worker in the same restaurant. They had a fight over his interest in the other woman. When she discovered that Hank had left her, Sandra was crushed. She had convinced herself that she loved him, though any outsider would have had no trouble seeing that they merely used one another. Soon, the shock of Hank's desertion turned into extreme anger. Then Sandra's anger turned into deep depression. She drank alone in the apartment for several days. Late one morning, she cut her wrists and waited to die. Instead, as she lay on the couch, she simply passed out. Because the cuts were not deep, the bleeding stopped by itself.

When the landlord came to her flat to collect the rent, he received no response to his knocking. He tried the doorknob and, when the door opened, he saw Sandra lying on the couch and blood on the carpet. He quickly phoned for help, and Sandra was taken to a hospital, where it was ascertained that she was in no danger of dying. After her wound was treated and she was detoxified, she was transferred to the psychiatric unit for evaluation and psychiatric treatment.

Sandra had brought no spiritual resources from her parental home when she left to live with Tony, who had been her first live-in companion. Both of her parents were strict born-again Christians. However, their insistence on strict rules of conduct aroused resentment in their daughter. Sandra rejected not only their religious beliefs, but also the moral values that they had tried to teach her. When Tony came along, she saw him as a way to escape from what she saw as a stifling religious atmosphere.

Her later separation from Tony was her idea when she met Hank. Tony had enabled her to get out of the parental household, but he had never really been her ideal. After a year, she was ready for a change. When Sandra told Tony that she wanted to live with Hank, it was Tony who had to nurse a broken heart. Sandra felt a twinge of pity, but only a twinge, which passed quickly. Her aim in both relationships was her immediate personal satisfaction, the same force which drove her abuse of alcohol and other drugs.

One Sunday morning, as she sat in the day room at the hospital watching television, she was exposed to a series of preachers telling her what they believed and that she ought to believe it too. There was little else to do on a Sunday morning in the psychiatric unit. The preachers spoke of faith in Jesus and Jesus' love for sinners. Since she did not see herself as a sinner, Sandra was bored.

While she was in treatment, Sandra was introduced to Alcoholics Anonymous. After several meetings, she was able to relate to other women who were recovering alcoholics. She was able to introduce herself by saying, "My name is Sandra and I am an alcoholic and drug addict." She acquired a sponsor, a woman named Sheila who had fifteen years of sobriety and a firm manner in her guidance of Sandra. When Sandra returned to her apartment, she found a job as a waitress and spent most of her evenings at A.A. meetings. Sheila led her through the first three Steps of the program of recovery.

The need to believe in a Higher Power continued to be an obstacle for Sandra. Sheila told her that she could make A.A. her Higher Power at the beginning. However, Sandra knew that Sheila's Higher Power who had kept her sober for fifteen years was God. By the end of the third month after her return from the hospital, Sandra was finally able to pray again. Because the only God she had ever known was Jesus, she began to pray to him. Morning and evening, she asked Jesus to keep her sober and to give her the humility to follow his lead in her life.

After nine months, Sheila told her to write out a moral inventory. She would review the bad and the good in her past life, and try to see her moral defects honestly. When she had completed her inventory a couple of weeks later, Sandra disclosed what she had written in a session with Sheila which lasted over two hours. At the same time, Sandra realized that she had to be honest with God. When Sheila left the apartment, Sandra sat quietly, asking Jesus' pardon for her many sins while she was using alcohol and other drugs. Then she reflected on all that the Lord had done for her in spite of the abortions, the sexual relationships which she knew had not pleased Jesus, and every other sin in her past life.

During her reflection, Jesus became more than a Higher Power who was convenient for her recovery. She was moved to a deep gratitude for his acceptance of her and his loving care during the past nine months. Sandra was finally able to abandon herself entirely to his love, to give her heart to him as he had given his heart to her.

A future that had been bleak when she was following only her own craving for sex and drugs on a path that led to death had become bright and hopeful. The future Jesus was offering her was the fulfillment of her deepest desires for life and love.

➳ PRAYER ☚

Lord Jesus, you send your Holy Spirit to restore and renew those who had ceased believing in you and who had given themselves over entirely to the power of their addictions. You came among people, many of whom had become enslaved by their desires. It was so then, and it is so today. From the beginning of your ministry among us, you proclaimed that you were a deliverer:

"The Spirit of the Lord is upon me,

because he has anointed me to bring good news to the poor.
He has sent me to proclaim release to the captives

and recovery of sight to the blind,

to let the oppressed go free,

to proclaim the year of the Lord's favor" (Lk. 4:18-19).

Unfortunately, we may have to come to nearly complete ruin before we wake up spiritually. What we see first is the ruin itself. Then we need a newfound faith that you are able and willing to deliver us. Finally, we have a choice between our old ways and a new way of life. Through it all you guide us with a tender, loving care. You lead us day by day closer to the wholeness that you want for us. You lead us closer to yourself, for you are the Power who can transform our lives and free us from all that might destroy us.

Because you have a heart that is tender and loving, the Sandras of this world can have hope, no matter how miserable their lives have become and how many times they may have offended you in the past. Be with them and all of us so that we may follow you faithfully until you bring us to our final deliverance in your everlasting embrace. Then we will thank you and praise you in the company of all whom you have set free:

> *The Lord sets the prisoners free;*
> > *the Lord opens the eyes of the blind.*
> *The Lord lifts up those who are bowed down;*
> > *the Lord loves the righteous....*
> *The Lord will reign forever,*
> > *Your God, O Zion, for all generations.*
> *Praise the Lord! (Ps. 146:7b-8, 10).*

Amen.

A YOUNG MAN IS DYING OF AIDS

Raymond was only thirty-five years old, but he looked much older. AIDS had sapped his strength and given him a haggard appearance. Lesions were already beginning to appear on various parts of his body. Getting up in the morning was a chore because of his bodily weakness. Medications that had worked for a while no longer seemed to be effective in slowing the progress of his disease. He could no longer hold down a job and depended on public aid for his support and medical treatment. He could look forward only to further decline until he died, as had so many before him. He was unlikely to live long enough to see a medical breakthrough. Raymond had lost several dear friends, and there were others who would not live more than a few years. He rarely saw them nowadays. He rarely saw anyone at all. He lived in his apartment like a hermit, going out only to do necessary shopping, and even that with great effort.

He knew that in some parts of the world his disease was an epidemic, that in large areas of Africa a huge number of people carried the AIDS virus and would die when the disease took hold. He pitied them because most of them would never even be offered treatment. He pitied himself, because they reminded him that he was becoming untreatable. Raymond tried not to wallow in self-pity because that would do no good. Still, it was hard to accept his fate.

Raymond had not contracted the disease through heterosexual activity, an accident as a health worker, a transfusion or even as a drug addict. He was a homosexual victim of AIDS and therefore doubly a pariah. Many people were uncomfortable around those who avowed a homosexual orientation, whether or not they were active. If they were active, there was often a deep aversion and deliberate avoidance. People saw AIDS in a homosexual as a judgment on his or her lifestyle. Moreover, there continued to be fear in the general population that even casual contact with an infected person could be contagious, in spite of overwhelming evidence to the contrary.

From his earliest years, Raymond's Catholic religious beliefs had always been conventional. He had been a morally troubled homosexual. The associate pastor at his parish had advised him to be celibate. On the wall of his apartment, Raymond had hung a painting based on a French wayside shrine. It depicted Jesus on the cross. The wound in his side, revealing the love in his heart, was clearly visible. It seemed to Raymond that the Lord was grieving over the sins of the world. The image portrayed a gentle Jesus, accepting of all humankind and of the suffering he bore for all humankind.

Sitting in a recliner before the painting, Raymond opened his Bible, which he read every day, and found the passage from Matthew's Gospel in which Jesus spoke about the choice Raymond would have to make:

But he said to them, "Not everyone can accept this teaching, but only those to whom it is given. For there are eunuchs who have been so from birth, and there are eunuchs who have been made so by others, and there are eunuchs who have made themselves eunuchs for the sake of the kingdom of heaven. Let anyone accept this who can" (Mt. 19:11-12).

Raymond realized that if he were to be faithful to what Jesus expected from him he would have to choose to let go of the homosexual activities which had led him to become infected with AIDS. He had never had any sexual interest in women. If he gave up his relationships with men, there would be nothing. He asked the Lord, "Why shouldn't I be allowed to have a sex life like everyone else? I haven't chosen to become a priest or a member of a religious order. Why should I have to live like one?" It didn't seem fair to him that being a eunuch was being thrust on him.

Then Raymond remembered that Jesus had never said that life would be fair. Indeed, in the Gospel which Raymond had just read, Jesus pointed out that some people have celibacy as their only option from birth. In other cases, men were mutilated against their will. There was nothing fair about either of these situations. All that Jesus ever promised was that those who were faithful to him and his word would find fulfillment in the kingdom of heaven. He said that the kingdom of heaven is in our midst, implying that the fulfillment begins even now because of his love for us. The Lord who loved him was clearly calling him to live like a eunuch, even though he had no desire to be one. What was he to do?

Raymond made the conscious decision to be a eunuch. And not just a eunuch, but a eunuch who was shunned because of his illness.

In ancient Israel, lepers were both shunned and condemned to a bleak future. In those days, leprosy included a variety of diseases that people feared. Once in a while, a leper would be healed. Many more spent their lives as outcasts. They were not allowed to enter towns and, in the countryside, they were required to call out "unclean, unclean."

Raymond turned to a passage from the Gospel of Matthew which described a healing by Jesus, showing his compassionate concern nor only for the physical distress of a leper but for his alienation as well:

> When Jesus had come down from the mountain, great crowds followed him; and there was a leper who came to him and knelt before him, saying, "Lord, if you choose, you can make me clean." He stretched out his hand and touched him, saying, "I do choose. Be made clean." Immediately his leprosy was cleansed. Then Jesus said to him, "See that you say nothing to anyone; but go, show yourself to the priest, and offer the gift that Moses commanded, as a testimony to them" (Mt. 8:1-4).

Raymond was struck first by the fact that Jesus actually touched a leper. That simply was not done at that time and place, because touching a leper would make Jesus ritually unclean. Raymond had had many opportunities to see how other people went out of their way to avoid touching not only him but anything he had touched, for fear they would be infected. When he meditated on this Gospel, Raymond came to believe that Jesus would not have hesitated to touch him for any reason.

The second item that Raymond noticed was Jesus' sending the leper to the priests. When they certified healing of the leprosy, the leper would no longer be a pariah. He could return to his family and the companionship of his friends and neighbors. The heart of

Jesus was quite sensitive to the leper's need for love and acceptance. Raymond believed that Jesus is still sensitive to this need in people today who suffer from AIDS.

Moved by this image of Jesus as well as the grieving figure on the cross, Raymond received the spiritual strength to decide to live each day as well as he could in harmony with Jesus' will for him. He resolved to confess his sins to the priest who had advised him to be celibate and to turn his life over completely to the care of the Lord. Jesus' heart understood him. Jesus would provide.

~ PRAYER ~

Lord Jesus, there are so many people who see themselves as aliens. People regard them as crazy persons or drunks or junkies or bearers of deadly diseases. They are lonely. They need love just as everyone else needs love. The book of Job describes what they feel:

"Do not human beings have a hard service on earth,
*   and are not their days like the days of a laborer?*
Like a slave who longs for the shadow,
*   and like laborers who look for their wages,*
so I am allotted months of emptiness,
*   and nights of misery are apportioned to me.*
When I lie down I say, 'When shall I rise?'
*   But the night is long,*
*   and I am full of tossing until dawn.*
My flesh is clothed with worms and dirt;

my skin hardens, then breaks out again.

My days are swifter than a weaver's shuttle,

and come to their end without hope" (Job 7:1-6).

Job suffered greatly from his afflictions. Everything in his life which had comforted him had been stripped away. He was sick and abandoned, as are so many modern aliens. He needed the love and understanding of those he had considered to be his friends. But that is not what they brought him. At the moment, there are many who have no one to console them. Yet they believe in you. You are not like other people. When they think about you touching the leper in the Gospel, they can easily imagine you touching them.

Abide with them now as they come to you in their loneliness. The peace in their hearts when you are near tells them that you come not to judge them but to be their friend and their savior. Perhaps their faith in you should be enough, but they are only flesh and blood, dear Lord. Therefore, I pray too that you may inspire someone with a compassionate heart to accept them as they are and offer the human companionship they need as a visible sign of your love for them.

On my own behalf and theirs, I thank you for the many times you have been patient when we wandered from you, leading us step by step out of darkness into the light of your truth. I thank you for forgiving us and showing us how much you love us. I thank you for your pledge that you will raise us above all our present difficulties to be united with you forever. Amen.

Chapter 6: Where Is God?

Over the course of a lifetime, some people lose faith in the God of heaven and earth. Often it is only a momentary loss. But loss of faith in God may be no more than a loss of faith in an *understanding* of God which is far removed from the truth. In Jesus, God revealed himself as a God of compassion and forgiveness. Yet some people insist on believing in a God who is rigid and severe. Others may not be able to believe in such a God and thus think that they have lost their faith. In fact, they may well be on the way to a better understanding and an authentic faith.

There is another way to lose faith in God where we continue to believe that God exists, but see God as One who is remote and impersonal, a God who does not respond to our suffering. Even those who believe that the Father has revealed his compassion in Jesus may have doubts when they need his compassion and cannot find him.

The supreme example of being tempted to ask, "Where is God?" is found in Jesus himself, hanging on the cross and uttering the words of the 22nd Psalm: "My God, my God, why have you forsaken me?"

The psalm continues:

Why are you so far from helping me,
from the words of my groaning?

O my God, I cry by day, but you do not answer;

and by night, but find no rest.

Yet you are holy,

enthroned on the praises of Israel.

In you our ancestors trusted;

they trusted and you delivered them.

To you they cried, and they were saved;

in you they trusted, and were not put to shame (Ps. 22:1-5).

The apparent abandonment of people who are not delivered from their persecutors has been called "the silence of God." Jesus chose to share our desolation, precisely because he is compassionate. His Father had not, in fact, abandoned him, nor does Jesus abandon us in our distress. Like Jesus, we may have to wait for God's response, and that response comes in a way which requires great faith.

In three days, Jesus would be raised from the dead. His suffering and resurrection would show us the way to the fulfillment of all our hopes. Through it all, God is near to us and very much concerned.

A MOTHER LOSES HER YOUNG DAUGHTER

The well-dressed matron in the waiting area of the surgical suite was furious. When the chaplain arrived to give her spiritual support, she turned on him with a vicious verbal assault, shouting:

"Why did this happen to me? I've been a good Catholic. I've always supported the Church. I've done everything a good Catholic is supposed to do. Why did God let this happen to my daughter? I wonder if there is a God. How could a God who is good let some fool shoot my little girl?" Looking at the chaplain who prudently said nothing, she added, "You tell me, where is God in all this?"

Charlene had indeed been an exemplary Catholic. In fact, she was a personal friend of the bishop and was considered a pillar of the Church in her diocese. She had devoted herself to many charitable causes, in which she drew other wealthy women into club activities that benefited the sick and the poor. She and her husband had also been principal contributors when Monsignor Sullivan sought funds to construct a new parish church.

Charlene's only child, a 20-year-old named Roseanne, had been hit by a stray bullet during a drive-by shooting incident among gang members. She and another young woman had been walking home from a movie at ten p.m. on a Friday evening when a car raced by and fired at a cluster of young people standing on a street corner. Most of the shots went wild and one struck Roseanne. Her companion, who carried a cellular phone, immediately called 911. Since they were downtown, it did not take long for paramedics to arrive.

When the ambulance brought her into the hospital emergency room, Roseanne was breathing and her heart was beating, but her blood pressure was extremely low. It was clear to the attending physician that the bullet had damaged a major blood vessel. He immediately sent her to an operating room for emergency surgery. Within minutes, a surgeon had opened her abdomen and blood gushed out. Because the vessel which had been hit by the bullet was deep among her organs in a pool of blood, and because she had lost much blood even during the quick trip to the hospital, he was not able to repair the damage before she died.

Her mother had arrived soon after Roseanne had been pronounced dead. Then the chaplain walked into the room and into the challenge of helping a bereaved mother who was very angry with God.

Charlene was asking the age-old question: "Why do the good suffer?" That question has been asked at innumerable bedsides, in the aftermath of war and persecution, and in many other settings in which we or our loved ones are suddenly afflicted or taken away. Many a Jew drew the conclusion that God was asleep during the holocaust—or that he did not exist. Many a child has lamented Jesus' deafness when losing a beloved parent or grandparent. The unexpected loss of a child, however, is particularly agonizing. Not only had Charlene lost a daughter; in a way, she had lost her own future.

Roseanne had been a good young woman. Charlene herself had done nothing to deserve the tragedy of her daughter's sudden death. The expectation of reward in this life for herself and her offspring is as old as the Bible. The psalmist said:

Mark the blameless, and behold the upright,
>	for there is posterity for the peaceable (Ps. 37:37).

Charlene saw herself as blameless and peaceable. Where now was her posterity?

For a Christian, the explanation of the mystery faced by Charlene is to be found in the passion, death and resurrection of Jesus. Matthew describes the scene as Jesus, God's Son, was dying on the cross:

> Those who passed by derided him, shaking their heads and saying, "You who would destroy the temple and rebuild it in three days, save yourself! If you are the Son of God, come down from the cross." In the same way the chief priests also, along with the scribes and elders, were mocking him, saying, "He saved others; he cannot save himself. He is the King of Israel; let him come down from the cross now, and we will believe in him. He trusts in God; let God deliver him now, if he wants to; for he said, 'I am God's Son'" (Mt. 27:39-43).

Jesus was the one of whom the Father had said on the bank of the Jordan, "This is my Son, the Beloved, with whom I am well pleased" (Mt. 3:17). He would hear these words again on the Mount of the Transfiguration.

Of himself, Jesus said: "...for I have come down from heaven, not to do my own will, but the will of him who sent me" (Jn. 6:38). Yet our savior, perfect in the eyes of his Father, deeply loved by him and always obedient, was allowed to die on the cross at the hands of the unjust. That was a scandal then and remains a scandal to this day.

But the cross was not the end of Jesus. Three days later God raised his Son from the dead as he had promised.

At the time of the death of Roseanne, Charlene was not ready to hear the message of the cross. Indeed, it would have been futile for the chaplain to have dwelt on this theme. At that moment, she needed time to work her way through her anger until she could come to acceptance of her loss.

Many months later, she made a three-day retreat designed to enable grieving people to accept loss and change in their lives. It was designed too to help them forgive those who had hurt them. For Charlene, that meant forgiving God. On its face the notion may seem preposterous. Yet, Charlene had been exceedingly angry with God. She needed to let go of that anger. She needed to accept God on God's terms.

The three-day retreat could only give her a point of departure in repairing her relationship with God. Over the following months, she prayed for and received the grace to believe that Jesus, who is both divine and human, did truly care about her and her daughter. She came to understand that the only way for any follower of Jesus is the path which he walked: suffering, which one day leads to resurrection.

With the healing of her emotional wound came greater humility and hope. Whatever persecutors or gang members may do in this world will be undone by the Lord. The present pain is passing; the consolation is eternal.

✦ PRAYER ✦

It can easily happen that we contemplate you hanging on the cross, Lord Jesus, and fail to see the obvious message for us in our lives. By any merely human reckoning you were a failure. Your work lay in ruins. Most of your followers had abandoned you. This happened to you in spite of the fact that you were the just one above all who are just. Why should it not happen to us?

No matter how good a Catholic or Protestant or Jew or any person may be, the good will of your Father does not mean that there will not be injustices inflicted on us and on those we love. You yourself and those closest to you were not exempt. It is true that persecution for our faith and accidental shooting are not the same. The first gives a religious witness; the second does not. However, the question "Where is God?" may arise in either circumstance. Why does God who is good and all powerful permit injustice? I believe that the only answer is the one given by St. Paul:

I consider that the sufferings of this present time are not worth comparing with the glory about to be revealed to us. For the creation waits with eager longing for the revealing of the children of God; for the creation was subjected to futility, not of its own will but by the will of the one who subjected it, in hope that the creation itself will be set free from its bondage to decay and will obtain the freedom of the glory of the children of God.... For in hope we were saved. Now hope that is seen is not hope. For who hopes for what is seen? But if we hope for what we do not see, we wait for it with patience (Rom. 8:18-21, 24-25).

The mystery of suffering is a mystery for a Christian as well as every-one else. Nevertheless, for a Christian it is a mystery with hope. The ulti-mate purpose of God is benign, as God has shown us in giving us the heart of his Son to be our consolation and salvation.

Therefore, I give you thanks, Lord Jesus, for every grace, including those which you give in our hour of grief. All of them flow from your cross and are a pledge of a future resurrection. Amen.

A Widow Mourns the Death of Her Son

Anna and her son Tom had lived together for many years. After the death of her husband, Anna had asked her unmarried son to leave his apartment and come to stay with her so that she would be less lonely. At that time she was seventy years old, and Tom had just turned forty. Mother and son got along very well together. Not only did they provide the companionship which both appreciated, but Tom was quite handy around the house. Ten years later, Tom was diagnosed with inoperable lung cancer. In six months, he was dead. Anna found herself completely at a loss when Tom died. She tried to adjust to living alone again, but after a couple of months, it was clear that she needed help. She went to visit her parish priest.

Father Leo was almost as old as Anna and, in fact, less able to get around than she was. The only reason he was still a pastor was that the bishop had no one to replace him. Thus, each day, he pushed his arthritic body through the labors of his ministry. A div-idend of his personal disability was great ease in understanding the problems of others. Anna rightly believed that if anyone could help her spiritually and emotionally, it would be Father Leo. At the funeral Mass, he had invited Anna to come to the rectory whenever she felt need of his moral support. She accepted his offer and went to visit with him.

They sat and talked in a comfortable lounge which Father Leo preferred for spiritual counseling. A large picture of the Sacred Heart of Jesus dominated the room. After asking Anna about her health and telling her about his own, they quickly got down to the reason for her visit. Anna's main difficulties since Tom's death had been a sense of total abandonment—no husband and no son—and lack of the physical help she needed around the house. Her story reminded Father Leo of a Gospel story which he read to her from a Bible lying on a table near his chair:

Soon afterwards he went to a town called Nain, and his disciples and a large crowd went with him. As he approached the gate of the town, a man who had died was being carried out. He was his mother's only son, and she was a widow; and with her was a large crowd from the town. When the Lord saw her, he had compassion for her and said to her, "Do not weep." Then he came forward and touched the bier, and the bearers stood still. And he said, "Young man, I say to you, rise!" The dead man sat up and began to speak, and Jesus gave him to his mother (Lk. 7:11-15).

When he had completed reading the passage, Father Leo told

Anna, "The Gospel tells us how deeply human Jesus is. He isn't going to raise Tom from the dead until we are all raised. Still, here and now, he is concerned about you. He has a heart for you as he had for that widow. He has a heart for you because you have suffered a great loss. He asks you to trust him."

The bereaved mother listened to the pastor and then replied, "Believing in Jesus is my only consolation now. I believe he will take care of Tommy. I hope he also takes care of me." She looked up at the picture of the Sacred Heart and immediately added, "I believe that he will take care of me, but it is so hard, Father."

She could see the concern in the pastor's eyes. "I am no substitute for your son," he said, "but I am always here for you. Any time you feel that you need to talk to someone who understands, I am ready to be your friend."

"Thank you, Father," she replied. "Your support is a great help to me. I think that Jesus sent me to you because he loves me. I trust him, and I know I can rely on you."

Father Leo gave Anna a blessing, and she went on her way less downhearted and more hopeful because she knew that she was never truly alone. Father Leo was nearby to comfort her, and Jesus was even closer, in her heart.

⤙ PRAYER ⤚

Lord Jesus, you have sent your Holy Spirit to your Church as its consoler. You also send your Holy Spirit to each of us in our personal need for the strengthening of our spirits. You yourself knew the grief of loss.

Tradition tells us that your father Joseph died sometime during your early years. He had loved you very much and you loved him. Scripture gives no record of that separation. Yet, because you have a human heart, you must have grieved deeply over the loss of his presence in your life and in your home. Your mother became a widow and you were able to feel her bereavement as well.

Throughout all time, you are close to widows and widowers. You are close to orphans and to friends who have lost companionship which had been especially dear to them. Death must indeed come to us all, and all of us will have to experience the loss of loved ones. We do not, however, have to bear this burden without hope, for you are near.

As Anna believed, you support us all by our faith in you. We believe that we will someday be reunited with one another in the kingdom of your Father. You gave this word to Martha outside the tomb of Lazarus:

Jesus said to her, "Your brother will rise again." Martha said to him, "I know that he will rise again in the resurrection on the last day." Jesus said to her, "I am the resurrection and the life. Those who believe in me, even though they die will live, and everyone who lives and believes in me will never die" (Jn. 11:25-26).

Lord Jesus, I pray for all of those who are grieving and who have great need of your consolation and support. I pray that I may be a help to them by my understanding and love. Be with us all as we journey toward everlasting union with you and reunion with our families and friends. Amen.

AN OLD MAN WHOSE WIFE HAS ALZHEIMER'S DISEASE

It didn't seem fair to Walter that he should be burdened with caring for Agnes. He had a weak heart and severe arthritis in his seventy-nine-year-old joints. Agnes, who was 78, no longer knew how old she was. Most of the time, it was not clear to her where she was. Walter doubted that she recognized him as her husband of fifty-five years. Her Alzheimer's disease was growing steadily worse. It would only be a few more months before Walter could no longer care for her and would have to place her in a nursing home. However, they would be long months, and he wondered how long he would last.

Sometimes, as he sat in a recliner looking over at her sitting on a sofa, staring blankly, he remembered the joyous events which had made their marriage a delight to him. He could see the young woman with whom he had fallen in love so very long ago. He could see the young mother caring for their first baby with instinctive skill when he was afraid even to hold his daughter, lest she break. He could see the lover whose caresses had comforted him and assured him of her love. The time of caresses had passed except when he might gently touch her cheek, but receive little response.

There was a shrine to the Sacred Heart in their parlor. Below a picture in which Jesus pointed to his heart, there was a table with a pair of candles, which he and Agnes had sometimes lit on religious feast days. Walter often looked toward the shrine and asked the

Lord how he could let Agnes deteriorate from a lively, loving human being into a vegetable. Why didn't he simply take her to himself?

Yet Walter's prayers were not answered. Agnes' general health was very good for an old woman. She might live for many more years as another blank face in a nursing home. Walter doubted that he would be around much longer in this world so that he could visit her. Nor would she be visited by their children. They were dispersed all over the world; the nearest, their daughter, lived 800 miles away and had her own family which needed constant attention. He wept when he thought of Agnes all alone, for the day would come when he was no longer alive.

Where was God in all this? He felt guilty about having such a thought. Yet it kept recurring whenever he looked first at Agnes and then at the picture in the shrine.

Walter realized that he had to live by pure faith. Agnes was not going to recover, and he was not going to become better able to care for her. Today he was still able to do so, and today was the only day he had. Tomorrow, others would do that for him. For the rest, tomorrow was entirely in the hands of God. Again and again, he brought himself to the point where he accepted these truths, though his grasp on them was weak and in need of frequent renewal.

He could feel what must have been in the heart of David when he sang:

How long, O Lord? Will you forget me forever?

How long will you hide your face from me?

    How long must I bear pain in my soul,

    and have sorrow in my heart all day long?

How long shall my enemy be exalted over me?

Consider and answer me, O Lord my God!

Give light to my eyes, or I will sleep

    the sleep of death,

    and my enemy will say, "I have prevailed";

my foes will rejoice because I am shaken.

But I trusted in your steadfast love;

    my heart shall rejoice in your salvation.

I will sing to the Lord,

    because he has dealt bountifully with me (Ps. 13:1-6).

Walter's enemies were the sorrows and labors of his home. There are countless households like that of Walter and Agnes. God is present in them, as is the heart of Jesus. Yet the presence is in the suffering itself. The model is the heart of Jesus pierced as he hung on the cross. What Jesus asks of Walter is heroic because his plan for both Walter and Agnes is endless joy beyond all human imagining. Walter's solace is his faith in that truth, a faith which he refreshes at moments of doubt and discouragement.

Once more, the old man rose from his chair and walked over to the old woman, gently brushing her cheek with his fingers. He would wait with patience for deliverance for both of them and a reunion in which their love for one another could not be dimmed by any earthly affliction.

-ᴽ P R A Y E R ᴦ

*Lord Jesus, all of us who are afflicted would do well to call to the Lord
as the psalmist did long ago, offering God our need and our faith in him:*

Out of the depths I cry to you, O Lord.

Lord, hear my voice!

Let your ears be attentive

to the voice of my supplications!

If you, O Lord, should mark iniquities,

Lord, who could stand?

But there is forgiveness with you,

so that you may be revered.

I wait for the Lord, my soul waits,

and in his words I hope;

my soul waits for the Lord

more than those who watch for the morning (Ps. 130:1-6).

*We can hear his reply in the words of another psalm, telling us of his
steadfast love:*

I sought the Lord, and he answered me,

and delivered me from all my fears.

Look to him, and be radiant;

so your faces shall never be ashamed.

This poor soul cried, and was heard by the Lord,

and was saved from every trouble.

The angel of the Lord encamps

around those who fear him,

and delivers them.

O taste and see that the Lord is good;

happy are those who take refuge in him.

O fear the Lord, you his holy ones,

for those who fear him have no want.

The young lions suffer want and hunger,

but those who seek the Lord

lack no good thing (Ps. 34:4-10).

Lord Jesus, be the daily support of those who care for their infirm spouses, parents, grandparents or children. With your grace, may they become able to place their difficulties and distress entirely into your hands. Your heart is full of kindness and compassion. I believe that after the suffering of this present time you will bring us all into your peace and joy.

Thank you for sustaining all of us during times of trial. I believe that your love has never abandoned us and will never abandon us and those whom we love. Amen.

Chapter 7: Immortal, Free and Destined for Glory

A little girl named Susie had a pet cat that she dearly loved. One day a car ran over her cat, and Susie was desolate. Her grandmother came to her, put her hand on her shoulder and said, "Susie, don't be so sad. Your little cat is happy in heaven with God." Susie looked up and asked, "Grandma, what does God want with a dead cat?"

Fortunately for all of us, whatever God may think about dead cats, God does want us. He wants us to find happiness with him. That is our hope, no matter what happens to us in this world. While we suffer personal loss in this world, we live by hope which grows out of our faith. When the heart of Jesus heals in this world, he is encouraging hope for a healing which is much greater than the particular healing for which we may pray. We cannot create this kind of hope by our own efforts alone. It is a grace, a free gift of God, which accompanies the gift of faith.

Prayer is a key to acquiring hope. It is in contemplating Jesus and his great saints, especially his mother, that we become filled with a confident assurance that Jesus will heal every wound. Jesus' Father sent him to be a savior to us. The Father loves us and asks for our love in return. He sends the Holy Spirit through Jesus to enable us to desire what he has promised and to be willing to follow his way to our fulfillment. Our fulfillment is to live in the love of the Father, the Son and the Holy Spirit. We suffer for a time; we love forever.

It is especially encouraging to a Christian that we believe in personal immortality. During Jesus' ministry, he was approached by Sadducees, who did not believe in the resurrection of the dead. They posed a problem relating to a woman who had been married to many husbands. They wanted to know whose wife she would be after the resurrection.

> Jesus answered them, "You are wrong, because you know neither the scriptures nor the power of God. For in the resurrection they neither marry nor are given in marriage, but are like angels in heaven. And as for the resurrection of the dead, have you not read what was said to you by God, 'I am the God of Abraham, the God of Isaac, and the God of Jacob'? He is God not of the dead, but of the living" (Mt. 22:29-32).

Moreover, when we have been raised, we will be free of all suffering. The book of Revelation tells us:

> "They will hunger no more, and thirst no more;
>> the sun will not strike them, nor any scorching heat;
> for the Lamb at the center of the throne will be their shepherd,
>> and he will guide them to springs of the water of life,
>> and God will wipe away every tear from their eyes"
> (Rev. 7:16-17).

We who have suffered for a short time in this world will be

filled with the Holy Spirit. One of the ancient names of the Holy Spirit is Glory. We will be filled with the Glory of the Lord, whose fruits are peace and joy.

Then we will sing in thanksgiving, together with the angels of God:

Praise the Lord!
Praise God in his sanctuary;
    praise him in his mighty firmament!
Praise him for his mighty deeds;
    praise him according to his surpassing greatness!
Praise him with trumpet sound;
    praise him with lute and harp!
Praise him with tambourine and dance;
    praise him with strings and pipe!
Praise him with clanging cymbals;
    praise him with loud clashing cymbals!
Let everything that breathes praise the Lord!
Praise the Lord! (Ps. 150:1-6).

⚬ PRAYER ⚬

Lord Jesus, you are the way, the truth and the life. Your way is the way of the cross, with the promise of resurrection. Your truth is the eternal love of your Father which has a long view of what is best for each of us—a share in your life of everlasting peace and joy after the troubles of the present time.

There is too much of us and not enough of you in how we live our lives now, Lord Jesus. At times we may forget that being loved by you does not mean that we and those dear to us will not suffer. Who has suffered more than your mother as she watched you die on the cross and be pierced with a lance?

By your grace, we know that you do not seek our suffering but rather our faith in you. It is by faith that we can overcome all suffering, whether our own or of those close to us. May our contemplation of your mother's sorrow along the way of the cross help us to see how much you have loved us all. We all need a share of her courage and faith.

I pray for all of the people to whom I minister that they may find in you the peace of mind and heart that they need in their service to you. They serve you when they serve one another. They serve you when they come close to you in your passion. They serve you by their faith, hope and love. May this book help them to give themselves over to your loving care. Bless them and bless me. Amen.

Remarkable stories of laity and religious who have found the loving, healing, and life renewing power of Jesus.

ENCOUNTERING JESUS IN THE GOSPELS AND DAILY LIFE

by Ronald Leinen, MSC

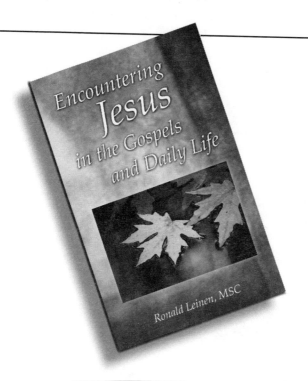

Other Books to Enrich Your Life and Share with Friends!

Why God Lets People Suffer
~Nancy C. Gaughan

How can a God of love allow suffering in the lives of his people?

Having experienced much suffering in her childhood and adult years, Nancy Gaughan shares her discovery in the Scriptures of God's reasons for allowing suffering in the lives of his people. It is her conviction that even in suffering's worst moments we can know joy and faith and trust in the God who loves us.

ISBN 0-9654806-5-8 paper $12.95

Jesus in the Image of God: *A Challenge to Christlikeness*
~Leslie B. Flynn

A great book for Bible study groups!

Here's a real antidote to the negative and faithless views of the Jesus Seminar. Let the Jesus of the Gospels challenge you to become more like him—the Son of God created in God's own image, who overcame despair, sorrow, rejection and humiliation to bring healing, redemption, hope, and the Good News of God's love to all human beings.

ISBN 0-9654806-1-5 paper $12.00